MITIGATING CIRCUMSTANCES

MITIGATING CIRCUMSTANCES

A DETECTIVE'S STORIES OF FORGIVENESS & THE FRUIT OF GOD'S LOVE

BRIAN D. BAKER

NASHVILLE

NEW YORK • MELBOURNE • VANCOUVER

MITIGATING CIRCUMSTANCES
A DETECTIVE'S STORIES OF FORGIVENESS & THE FRUIT OF GOD'S LOVE

© 2017 **BRIAN D. BAKER**

Published in New York, New York, by Morgan James Publishing. Morgan James is a trademark of Morgan James, LLC. www.MorganJamesPublishing.com

The Morgan James Speakers Group can bring authors to your live event. For more information or to book an event visit The Morgan James Speakers Group at www.TheMorganJamesSpeakersGroup.com.

ISBN 978-1-68350-254-8 paperback
ISBN 978-1-68350-256-2 eBook
ISBN 978-1-68350-255-5 hardcover
Library of Congress Control Number: 2016915847

Cover Design by:
Rachel Lopez
www.r2cdesign.com

Interior Design by:
Bonnie Bushman
The Whole Caboodle Graphic Design

In an effort to support local communities, raise awareness and funds, Morgan James Publishing donates a percentage of all book sales for the life of each book to Habitat for Humanity Peninsula and Greater Williamsburg.

Get involved today! Visit
www.MorganJamesBuilds.com

DEVOTION

I devote this book to my wife and daughter. Together, their loving patience toward me is what makes life valuable. I love what God has done in our lives together.

CONTENTS

ACKNOWLEDGEMENTS

I especially want to thank God for being right there when I turned to Him and asked Him to fill my heart. He gave me the ability to empathize and to love and to write. As my walk with God strengthened, so did my ability as an investigator.

My mother loved God more than I ever understood. Part of my own personal healing has been a realization that Mom planted seeds of God's love in me and that she had faith that someday I would be all right. I think about my mom all the time even though she died almost 15 years ago. She would be proud to know that I love God too, and she would love the book and the accounts of my profession.

My wife Michelle deserves big recognition for editing and for helping to bring a scriptural consistency to the chapters. We strived to make the passages relevant without being preachy. She focused days of attention into scriptures of encouragement. A book about what God has done without including some of God's Word is out of balance. Even if you aren't walking with God or you are reading this from a different spiritual view, we hope that you will see the encouragement in God's Word. Michelle believed that by adding these specific Scripture passages, the reader would have a lead on something to pass along to another brother or sister who needs a place to start thinking about God…to start healing.

In 2003 I met Eugenie Rayner while we attended the Master of Arts program at Vermont College in Montpelier, Vermont. Genie went on to become a respected editor and well-known regional writer in the Bennington area. She helped me greatly with the professional edits and formatting of this book. I am looking forward to future work with Genie on my team.

My interest in writing and creativity grew out of my Vermont College experience. I was the only criminologist during the academic semesters, and during colloquium time, my best friends were the "creative people." Even then I was telling detective stories, and although I didn't walk with God at that time, God's Spirit was certainly over our lives in that program. My Vermont College creative friends always said I was an artistic person, an inspirational writer, a storyteller… that I was a "creative" and just didn't know it yet. I want to thank those friends for encouraging me.

I want to thank my faculty advisors, Margaret Blanchard and Rochelle Ruthchild, and my mentors from Vermont College for their help and devotion to my success. Without them I could not have accomplished my educational goals of becoming an expert in my field and an educator for the next generation. The happiness I have enjoyed as an adjunct criminology instructor at Penn State is rooted in my Vermont College degree. My education qualified me to be involved in most of the cases and profiles I write about in this book, and I am grateful for that.

While at Penn State, I had the distinct honor to become acquainted with writer and associate professor of English, Toby Thompson.

In 2009, my wife and I enjoyed his graduate course in memoir and creative non-fiction. After many years, the itch to write, or to learn how to write better, was finally scratched. After that semester, I had a deeper desire to write, but I ignored it for many years. That itch, I finally realized, was a tickle from God to write my stories, so I went back to Toby Thompson for another semester of memoir and a third semester to learn to write biographical profiles. Toby has been a great mentor, encourager, and friend.

Another great writer who has been a role model and source of encouragement is Cecil Murphy. I met Cecil in 2014 while at a Christian Counseling conference with my wife. He was inspirational to me, because he and I had similar childhood experiences, and we were both passionate about writing and storytelling. Cecil is widely published. He offered a scholarship that helped me to afford my first Christian Writer's Conference. When I met Cecil outside one of the conference sessions and I told him how significant the experience was to me, he hugged me with gladness. His words of encouragement and his example as a Christian writer who is open-hearted and sincere have never left me.

There have been several attorneys who have trusted me with investigations, but even more important was their reliance on my words and perspective to complete mitigation profiles and help with sentencing advocacy for clients. Attorneys can get a bad rap for being mercenary, immoral, and sleazy. I've been fortunate in my career to have the discernment to be cautious who I work with and what I do. One of the benefits of being a consulting detective is the ability to pick my clients and control my schedule and to control those boundaries. Our justice system is unique in the world because of a presumption of innocence. Criminal defense attorneys are necessary to guide these offenders' cases through the justice system to preserve the liberties and rights our justice system affords. While I don't spend much time in this book discussing my experiences working with attorneys—maybe that would be a good book for the future—I would say the majority of my attorney clients have been cordial in their working relationship with law enforcement, sensitive to the impact of the crimes upon the victims, and empathetic toward the themes and life experiences of the offenders they represent.

My friends Stephanie and Scott Walters, and my administrative support person, Mandie Buxton, have been excellent contributors to this book project. Thank you to Stephanie for reading and contributing corrections and suggestions for clarity. Thanks also go to Mandie for helping with research and for her work on my social media and Website.

I've been reconnected with my cousin Landon Laub only a few short years. I've missed so much of what an interesting large family experience could have been, but through knowing Landon, I have learned the family history I need to know. Maybe we can look at the years with some comedy instead of regret and believe that God has a sense of humorous efficiency where He gives us only what we can appreciate and in the timing He decides is right. I won't spoil the ending of the book, but undoubtedly God put Landon and me together for reasons, and one of those reasons was to know our cousin Linda. Linda, in our short acquaintance, filled in many more gaps about the family I didn't know and some of the history of my dad's life that made him what he was to me. Linda has had a lifelong walk with God, and her faith and love of God are inspirational to me. She knows God and therefore knows that what is not God is of the enemy. I'm glad to be able to tell some of Linda's story here. I look forward to being able to tell the rest of her story very soon.

These stories have been altered to protect the privacy of the men and women I write about. The criminal offenders in these stories have done some horrific acts that some people might believe are impossible to forgive and recover from. But these are stories of forgiveness, and I want to thank the offenders I have worked with and their families. You have all helped my faith and my growth and my relationship with God.

I want to thank the team at Morgan James Publishing: Managing Editor Tiffany Gibson, David Hancock, Jim Howard, and especially Acquisition Editor Terry Whalin for his persistence and interest in my stories.

Lastly, I want to thank you, the reader, for understanding these men and women and not compounding their shame with judgment.

There is a difference between encouraging crime and understanding crime. I encourage every reader to proceed with an open heart toward each story and to be slow to judge. Each case is a public tragedy, and although there are individual victims and the family members who survive, crime hurts us all because it is an offense against our personal peace.

Ernest Hemingway once said, "As a writer you should not judge. You should understand." The Bible, too, warns us not to judge others hypocritically (Matthew 7:3-5). My greatest satisfaction as a private detective, criminologist, educator, and writer, then, is the ability to explain crime so that others can not only understand the actions and misdeeds of the offenders, but also extend grace and forgiveness.

Preface

FOR THE LEAST OF THESE

When I was young, my mother told me a story that ended with Jesus telling his disciples, "Whatever you do for the least of your brothers and sisters you do for me." She told variations of this story to me more than once, the last time when I was a senior in high school. I didn't know God at all during those high school days or for many years after. Though my mom loved God, it wasn't until after she died that I fully grasped how her own life of caring, service, and quiet philanthropy was truly a mission that mirrored this parable about the sheep and the goats in Matthew 25.

My mother didn't just love that parable. She lived it. People approached me after her death to relay stories about her monetary gifts to the town library and her church. Another organization told me that, for years, my mother supported children by purchasing winter coats for them and paying for their medical expenses. I learned from her pastor that she had devoted time each week to help in the church office and that she was a reliable giver to special projects or missions. And like Jesus said in Matthew 6:3 about giving to the needy—do not let your left hand know what your right hand is doing—my mom didn't draw attention to her giving to impress others. She gave to others in secret, so that only she and God knew. So humble and quiet was her giving, it wasn't until after her death that I, her only child, knew how generous she was and how much that generosity meant to others.

Now, more than a decade after she died, I wish that she knew of my relationship with God, inspired so much by how she lived her own. Unfortunately, she didn't live long enough to witness my transition to a life of faith. She knew me as a young man who was hurting, angry, and confused because of the abuse I had suffered at the hands of my father. But after I was born again, and I first read the parable of the sheep and the goats in the Gospel of Matthew, I remembered how she would paraphrase that story for me. I was thunderstruck at not only how this parable defined my mom's love for God, but how its principles guided the work she had done for others.

Since my own spiritual awakening, I consciously see the importance of my own work—my vocation as a professional investigator—serving the least of our brothers and sisters by bringing truth, accountability, understanding, vindication, and fellowship.

I'm the guy who visits people in prison.

Sometimes I become their last friend on this earth. In my cases, I am strongly led by God to minister to both the accused and convicted, and He has helped me to understand and empathize with them, as well as with the families who suffer in the confused wreckage of a life gone off course.

My stories are not easy. Who do I envision reading these stories? Families of people in prison. Friends of juvenile delinquents. Others who minister to inmates. Those who like a good detective story. Inmates themselves. Who am I concerned about who may read these stories? The sweet grandmother who has led Sunday school for twenty years and lives on a quiet street and has never had anything bad happen to anyone she knows. I cringe as I imagine her, and innocents like her, shuddering at the raw violence I can't entirely sanitize from these accounts. Please know that any such details are not gratuitous. I include them so that readers can understand the lives of the people I help to defend and marvel at how much God has changed them.

This book arose from the many friends and students who heard these stories and said, "You should write a book." So I did. But I'm not a religious professional. I've worked as a private investigator for over 25 years, and since I turned to God, the meaning and value of my work has changed incredibly. Consequently, this book is a way for me to commemorate the amazing things God has done for convicted men and women during my career. Like the blind man whom Jesus healed, all I can say is that I once was spiritually blind, but now I see; after meeting Jesus, my life is completely new (John 9:25). And with that newness, I've found that my cases have taken on much greater importance. I care more deeply about what happens to everyone involved, including the criminal offenders, their families, and their victims.

Of course the people I work with have their own beliefs, or lack of beliefs. I am not one of those guys who slips a Bible verse into every phone call or who says goodbye with "have a blessed day." But when the time is right, I won't hesitate to pray for someone. My world view is realistic but not so crowded by tragedy or political correctness that I won't speak God's Word.

In my profession, I meet many distraught people, and I pray for peace in their heart. Those are my exact words. I pray this in jails; I pray this in courtrooms; I pray this on the front porches of the homes of victims and family members. Ultimately, I'm praying for God to help these people rise above the anxiety, pain, and devastation that their actions, or the actions of someone else, have caused. I have prayed this with many people, and God has responded to those prayers, as well as to the prayers of others associated with these cases.

I am only able to pray for peace in others' hearts, though, because God has first put peace in my heart. I was born again in 2009, and my relationship with Jesus has influenced how I see both myself and the offenders I work with. Because the change God has made in my heart has had such an impact on my casework and how I work with offenders, I begin this book with a brief narrative of my own testimony.

I also pray that as you read this book, God will meet you and speak to you. He is a perfect Father who will never hurt you, abandon you, or set you up for failure. God won't mock your fears or humiliate you for His own entertainment. Unfortunately, many of the fathers of the offenders in these stories did exactly these things. Once these offenders met Jesus, however, they found a heavenly Father who is sober, loving, faithful, and kind.

They found a Father they could trust, and His perfect love changed their lives forever.

In the rawness of their hard lives, God showed up and proved just how much He loves them, despite their failures.

And isn't that the way He shows up for all of us? Our failures may differ from person to person, but we've all fallen short of perfection. Every single one of us.

We all need God's grace, and these are the stories of God's great grace.

I hope their stories touch your heart the way they touched mine.

CHAPTER 1
PRETEXT

"Therefore, if anyone is in Christ, he is a new creation. The old has passed away; behold, the new has come."
—2 Corinthians 5:17

The PI business takes patience…and a lot of courage. I sit in hot cars all day, sometimes up to sixteen hours at a time. Most of the time, I'm crunched in the backseat, peering with a camera through homemade window coverings or tint that's too dark by police standards. My doctor said the muscles in my back are knotted like a spiral telephone cord because of the hours I've spent jammed in the back of cars. The first time I felt real terror, I was hiding in the backseat on surveillance, staring through the window at the barrel of a revolver. It was gripped in the hand of a drug dealer curious to know if anyone was behind the tint…and why.

I also talk to angry people. Very angry people. People who threaten me if I call them or set foot on their property again. People who resent and resist being handed subpoenas. People who insist they've done nothing wrong—that they were framed, falsely accused, or misunderstood. People who first learn that a private investigator was following them when I take the stand and testify that they're guilty. Though I help a lot of people, I make a lot of people angry. One such man was so angry he stood at the edge of my backyard with a rifle trying to get a clear shot at me. He had recently been released from prison, but I had helped to put him behind bars.

Thank God for the thick covering of trees around that house.

The only reason I knew about this attempt on my life is because another angry offender told me about it: "We don't see eye-to-eye, Brian, but I don't play like this," he said. "That ain't right. You're just doing your job."

Just doing my job seems to get me into a lot of trouble.

When I'm not surveilling or infuriating people, I support this field work with painstaking research: scrolling through computer records at a snail's pace; standing for hours at the counters of clerks of court reading transcripts; wading through boxes of discovery; listening to hundreds of hours of recorded phone conversations; and hoping I don't have nightmares after viewing grisly autopsy and crime scene photos.

Not as sexy as the movies make it, huh? And not as safe, either. In film, there's a director who can say "cut," the blood is fake, and the detective knows what the villain is going to say next. Film detectives can also take more dramatic risks, because their bullet-proof vests don't have to stop real bullets, their stunt doubles take all their falls, and they don't have the real law to uphold.

Maybe the intriguing part, if there is one, is when we employ deception to convince others to talk to us—something like Chevy Chase's character in the 1980s movie, *Fletch*. In PI parlance, this deception is known as a pretext, or the cover story you create to get information you could not otherwise have known. For a pretext to work, you need to be part actor, part stuntman, and part delinquent.

Rule number one for a pretext is to know when to stop (unlike Fletch).

Rule number two is directly related to rule number one: don't break the law.

Police pretexts are called stings, and if you are the one who is stung, then you might call it entrapment. Criminal pretexts are known as scams or cons. When normal people use a pretext, it's called a lie. Most normal people I've met operate under some form of pretext in their lives—some persona or ideal self they shove out into the world and then hide behind.

This is part of what makes my job so hard: everyone lies, or so it seems.

As a detective, there are two styles of professional pretexts—active and passive. We call them a cover story or a front. In active pretexts, I'm usually going after someone on their turf.

I ring a doorbell, show a photo of a puppy, and ask, "Has anyone seen my dog?" Based on who answers the door, I know who lives there and if they are home.

I approach someone in the parking lot of a grocery store and ask, "Sir, would you be interested in a shopping spree?" Then I watch to see if the supposedly injured claimant, who is on disability, dead lifts hundreds of pounds of groceries into his car. I make sure not to stand in front of the surveillance van at the end of the parking lot that is capturing it all on film.

Or I offer to sell someone a shipment of stolen motor oil (it's not really stolen) and see if they bite.

In passive pretexts, I wait for them to come to me—though I hope they don't.

If I do surveillance in my own vehicle, strangers will approach and angrily ask, "Why have you been sitting outside my house all morning?" If I show that stranger a photo of a plain white tractor trailer, I can use that truck to invent five different stories as to why I'm sitting there. Even better, if I put decal letters on my car door that spell out "ROAD SURVEY," and I make sure the letters are on straight, I'm so obvious, I'm invisible.

For a while, I used a school photo of one of my operative's nieces as a pretext. One Saturday, I was parked at a body shop in a bad neighborhood when the owner and his wife surprised me. I flashed my detective badge and a photo of the child, and before I could form my words, the woman burst into tears and the man was ready to hand me the keys to his door.

"You can park here all day," he said, trying to console his wife. "I'm sorry to bother you."

I hate upsetting people with pretexts, but, as the man said, I'm just doing my job.

I used to pretext banks: tell the bank I was cashing a check for someone, give a name and birth date, and ask if they had enough money in their account to cover twenty dollars. Tellers would put me on hold and come back and say, "Yes, sir, that check is good," or "No, sir, that account closed and the funds were transferred to another bank.... Confirm the address? Why yes, sir, just a minute....What is the name of the receiving bank? Sir, the name of that bank is…"

Pretexting a bank is now a federal crime.

Over the years, though, most pretexts, and the situations for those pretexts have not changed. Everything else has. Cameras have gotten smaller. Guns are mostly plastic. Videotape morphed into DVD and then evaporated into the cloud. Cell phones were the size of bricks and weighed about as much. Now phones do the same thing as computers, and you can still talk on them. Smoking cigarettes turned into vaping. Thank God I quit.

We used to carry rolls of quarters for the payphone, and when we'd find a payphone in use, we'd back up our car, get the tailpipe as close to the phone booth as possible, and let the engine exhaust smoke the person off the phone.

If I wanted a photo of someone, I figured out who they were and then I took their photo. With a camera. And film. Sometimes I took a lot of photos and then went back to the clients and asked them to pick the right person so I could continue the investigation.

Not anymore. Most people have photos of themselves, their house, their pets, their children, their car, their friends, the food they ate for breakfast, their favorite TV shows, and their most recent vacation posted on social media, updated practically by the minute, ready for me to screen capture and use. Days spent canvassing a neighborhood for pieces of information have been replaced by clicking through social media and the White Pages online. The "all about me" social media phenomenon has been a boon for PIs doing open source intelligence searches. I once tracked down a man based on the photo of his car on social media. I needed to locate his house, but the address history I had was no good. All I knew was that he lived along a particular highway and drove a white car. The photo of the car on social media included the license plate, and because I knew the general area where he lived, I drove around looking for the car. When the car passed by me, with his father driving the vehicle, I saw the license plate number in my rearview mirror. I made a u-turn and followed the car back to my subject's house. All thanks to social media.

Film noir romanticizes the shady, unethical, quasi-legal deeds of the detective, while in reality, such things as picking a lock, reading someone's mail, trespassing, or muscling somebody would put the real licensed PI out of business or behind bars. Though pretexting is legal (within limits), it still didn't feel like reputable work to me, and there were plenty of people willing to let me know that.

In my hometown, a retired cop named Frank advertised his private investigation services in the Yellow Pages and ran an office out of the old city hotel. It was a Sam Spade or Philip Marlowe style office, with a gritty view of the street and the detective's name painted on the door. Frank was a nice guy, but he was physically slow and this cheapened his wisdom and soft skills in the eyes of the county bar association. While I didn't fashion myself as a smartass like Spade or Marlowe, I had to hold back whenever someone compared me to Frank. They didn't mean it with any respect—to me or to him.

Likewise, in college, a professor asked the class what each of us wanted to do with our lives after graduation. When it was my turn to share, I replied that I wanted to be a licensed private detective and have my own firm. I wanted to help others who couldn't help themselves. I wanted to help people know the truth. The professor smirked and told me I was a waste of a good education. He thought it was a shame I didn't have higher goals.

The voice was the professor's, but the words sounded just like my dad, as if my dad had encouraged him to humiliate me. The only thing missing in that classroom was getting kicked off my chair or getting my nose bloodied in front of my friends. Another disappointment tattooed inside my heart, and here I was powerless and unable to help myself. I let the prof's poison float around the classroom like swamp gas and no one else said a word.

Even before grade school, I never knew when my dad would hit me next. It might be in the yard for not walking fast enough or at the dinner table for not eating a Brussels sprout. I only knew it was coming. I can still recall how far my angry father could throw a Big Wheel. Surprisingly, that bike was unbreakable. I was not.

When I was ten years old, I woke up to an empty house on a cold Sunday morning. No one was home and it was unusual, scary. I waited without eating breakfast or watching TV or turning on a light. Had I done anything besides wait, I could be struck. Then our car pulled in and my dad was alone.

"Where's Mom?" I asked.

Three stiff words were his reply: "Your grandma died."

He brushed past me without removing his coat and disappeared somewhere in the house. I held my breath and stayed out of his way. Later he left the house, and I was free to scream my anguish to the empty rooms. I felt lost because I loved my mom's mother. I'd known Grandma was sick my whole life, but I never really understood death—just that death was the end. I hugged the dog, who didn't flinch at my sorrow, and when I repeated the words "no one loves me now," the dog surely disagreed.

That pain had never left me, even after I grieved Grandma's passing. There would be years of feeling sad for the deaths of other family members and friends, feeling scared to the point of insomnia and anger. I never knew what was going to happen next. Who was going to hit me? What bad circumstance would knock me over? I knew one thing for sure: I was unsatisfactory, full of bad ideas and that nothing was right—that I wasn't right. After years of being hit, my dad had knocked the "common sense" into me that I was no good, unlovable, and worthless. Sadly, I believed it deep down into the core of who I was.

Still, as an adult, I managed to walk and maintain the pretext of a cool young PI who had it all together.

When carrying a badge, I also carried anger and a lack of confidence. I pretended. I acted. And it worked on the street. I liked testifying in court—something few people enjoyed—because I knew if I just told the truth, I would be safe there. Even though my mom had said she loved me, and I believed her, that truth hadn't shielded me from the ongoing abuse from my dad.

I couldn't understand why my mom wouldn't defend me from him. Instead of defending me, she tried to tell me it was normal for fathers to "be like that." But I could tell she didn't believe it. Her dad had lived inside a bottle, so the only thing missing for her were the visible bruises. I would tell her my other friends didn't get shoved to the ground and kicked at Little League practice, but she would busy herself with something else or tell me to go outside and play.

Compared to a lot of men I've met as a detective, I was lucky my dad was physically weak. He never chained me up and whipped me, the way some fathers did when they made parole. He never whaled on me like a prize fighter. It was usually just a few surprise blows or a kick in the ass and a shove. I didn't ride a bus to school, so I was spared the humiliations at the bus stop that some men had experienced as boys, as you will find in a later chapter. And thankfully my dad didn't hit my mom. He would shout and curse at her, but he didn't hit her. Because she only told a few friends about his behavior, few people would have believed my father capable of such abuse.

For as long as I knew him, my dad operated under a pretext. He presented himself as a friendly, easy-going family man with a successful business and a happy home life, but I knew differently. At home he was cruel, cold, critical, and dangerous to be around, both physically and emotionally.

He was good at covering things up; in fact, he did it for a living. He sold carpet, paint, wall coverings, blinds, and curtains. He learned the upholstery and furniture trade after his father abandoned him and his mother when he was fourteen years old. His brothers and sisters were all grown with families of their own, so manhood was his problem to figure out. He worked after school in an upholstery shop down the alley from his house, and it grew into his life's work.

Oddly, my father didn't count on my getting bigger—much bigger. By the time I was fifteen, I was no longer a victim, but an opponent. One afternoon, I was eating lunch in the kitchen with my mom when he started yelling angry questions at us. He didn't like an answer I gave, and he began screaming and flailing his arms, a sure sign that he was about to strike.

When he moved forward to hit me, I pushed my chair back, assumed a fighter's stance, and said, "Go ahead, let's fight."

Shocked, he backed down and that was the day the physical abuse ended. After that, his abuse switched from physical violence to complete neglect, and he virtually never spoke to me again. I carried a painful, anxious feeling in my chest until the calendar ran down and I left home for college.

I graduated from college, got married, and began my PI business. About ten years later, I became a father. During that time, I mimicked my father's pretexting skills to create the façade of a happy life: Wife, kid, my own business, a decent house, a graduate degree, and a teaching appointment at a college. From the outside, everything looked fabulous, but I was miserable. Absolutely miserable. No material blessing could take away the deep shame I felt. I had been beaten, ridiculed, and made a fool of my whole life, and I was furious about it. I hated my father. At that point, the only person I felt who truly loved me was my mother.

When she was diagnosed with cancer, I was devastated. Less than twenty-four hours after that diagnosis, she died. Once again she told me she loved me, this time as I held her in my arms on a hospital bed. Those were her last words to me.

At Mom's funeral, Dad did not cry. He tried to sob but couldn't make tears. He tried to talk sorrowfully, but it was self-centered. People would attempt to hug him, but he hated it. He needed her as part of the pretext. She was the one who was elegant and emotional.

For a few years after my mom died, with the help of abundant amounts of alcohol, I maintained my pretext until my first wife told me in the heat of an argument that I was just like my father. Though I was not physically abusive to anyone, I was angry all the time, cynical, sarcastic, and hateful to people. She had no idea how badly I hated my father, and I hated what I had let him do to my life. A few weeks later, she and I were separated, and from that moment, I vowed to become a better person so I could be a better dad to my child than my father was to me. My marriage may have been destroyed, but I would not allow my relationship with my child to be destroyed along with it.

Being a PI didn't help my relationships. I had experienced so much vicarious pain through crime victims, had rubbed shoulders with so many hardened criminals, and had become so reclusive, that I believed all people were like the people I had helped to incarcerate. I didn't like to talk about the fear, uncertainty, and helplessness that my job created, so I stuffed it deep down, hid it behind my pretext. I found myself becoming emotionally numb to manage the pain. Because I wouldn't let myself feel pain, I couldn't feel joy, either. Somehow, I had shut down entirely. My happiness rarely broke through the ice of anger, unless there was booze or laughter or the thrill of a chase involved.

I lived by pretexts, and this felt normal.

Remember rule number one about pretexts? Know when to stop.

My dad never said "I love you." Unfortunately, I've found that plenty of guys' dads never said that to them. My dad and I both wasted so much of our lives hating almost everything and everybody, and as adults we were nasty to our wives, who resented us for it.

I ended the pretext, separated from my wife, and left town. Now, as a Christian, I know that was the wrong choice, but at the time, I didn't know God. Sadly, I didn't even *want* to know God. In my mind, God the Father was someone who didn't have time for me, who wasn't trustworthy. Fathers were hateful and abusive. That was all I believed.

Like another man whom you will meet in this book, if I had known God, I wouldn't have been in the mess that I was in.

After some time, I met a woman who was a Christian. She had experienced significant church abuse for more than a decade and was not attending any church. We quickly fell in love, but we were both skeptical of organized religion. We had no idea that God was drawing us both toward Him and toward a healthy church family. A few years later, we got married, and on the same evening, in the very same spot that we said our vows, I repented and confessed that I believed Jesus to be my Savior and Lord. For the first time, I felt God's Spirit in my heart along with a peace I had never experienced before.

In that moment, I finally realized something so many other men and women mistrust: God the Father is not like my earthly father. This Father loves while my earthly father destroyed. My wife and I started going to church together, and, over time, He brought everything I had hidden behind my pretext into the light so that my heart could be healed. I saw myself in the grievous wrongs and abuses that Jesus bore for us on the cross. I knew that I was a sinner saved by God's grace, and for the first time in my life, I was joyous and it wasn't a pretext.

As I began to grow as a Christian and read the Scriptures, I found God's rule number one: love God. That seemed easy enough—God was perfect, holy, kind, generous, and compassionate. How could I not love Him?

Then I read God's rule number two: love your neighbor as yourself.

To Jesus, these "neighbors" included unlikely characters, such as enemies. I was supposed to pray for people who persecuted me (Matthew 5:44). To intensify this, I found in Scripture that people who said they loved God but didn't love others were deceiving themselves (1 John 4:7-12). Their love for God was a pretext.

This is when God began moving on my heart to forgive my dad.

It wasn't immediate. I argued with myself a lot and some with God. I wrote stories about my life and what my dad had done to me. I prayed about my anger and the fallout from his abuse. I told my pastor and friends that I was praying against anger and unforgiveness, weakness, and shame, and they supported me with their own prayers. I talked about it with my wife, and she helped me to see behaviors and fears that were all a result of my scars.

Then I shared my story with my young daughter. She told me that I had changed, and it was exciting that she had seen this transformation in me. I suddenly realized what God's Spirit had accomplished in my life, something I had wanted for many years: God had taken away my sins, pain, shame, and unforgiveness; with those things, He took away the reality that I would become just like my father. I did not need to worry that my daughter would not love me. I told her that I forgave my father. Later I would confess this to my men's group at church and to my extended family, and then to strangers and to my enemies. When my dad died, I felt free not because he was gone but because, with his departure, I had forgiven him.

Over the years, the cases I've worked on have changed and so have the pretexts. They're gone. I've enjoyed the ability to tell the truth: to knock on a door, hand someone my card, and show my badge. I tell them plainly why I am there and what I want. Because God has healed my heart, I'm not riddled with shame and am much more secure in His love. In my career, this has translated to my taking more challenging cases, traveling more extensively, learning new skills, speaking at conferences, and training young PIs and security professionals. God's love has also given me the courage to stand in front of classrooms full of hundreds of undergraduate students and teach them about crime theories and the criminal justice system. Unlike my discouraging professor, I'm able to mentor them; invite many of them for big Italian dinners at my house, courtesy of my wife; and help them not only in their careers, but spiritually as well. I never thought I would be able to mentor young people this way.

Not only has my teaching taken on new meaning, but my investigative work has, too. God has given me discernment during interviews to know what questions to ask and how to ask them. As a result, men have confessed their crimes to me, and I've helped them to take responsibility for their actions. An important result of these confessions is that they keep victims from the pain and humiliation of testifying during trials—few people know the depth of their stories. Additionally, I've been able to help offenders emotionally, so they don't pull the trigger on themselves when they are depressed or regretful about their crimes or prison sentences.

This was how I put my education to good use: God drew me to Him, and I responded by repenting and believing in Him; He forgave me, and in doing so, He enabled me to forgive others, even those who hurt me the worst, like my father. As an outgrowth of His Spirit working in my life, my character changed, and because of that, the nature of my career changed. With God's help, I now help others, both in the criminal justice system and, more importantly, in their spiritual lives.

I'm so glad I no longer live behind a pretext.

One of the hardest parts of having a pretext is when it is ripped off, like a mask exposing your true identity, or a Band-Aid on an infected wound. I found that my dad's pretext was torn away as he lay dying. His brother, who never knew the extent of my father's anger, went to visit him one last time to bring the Good News about salvation to him. My dad cursed his brother out the door—a gale force of the rage and fury he had felt for more than sixty years. The last hours of his own cancer death could have been blessed with the peace of forgiveness and salvation, but instead of allowing God to take away his anger, my dad chose not to repent, and he carried those bitter feelings with him to the grave.

Dad chose to barely be remembered, making his passing almost invisible. He had made prearrangements for his memorial, which was limited to cremation followed by a burial next to my mother. The poorly written obituary, in which my name was spelled incorrectly, did mention his life's work, his business selling home interior supplies. The facts about his family may have been wrong, but his legacy of covering things up was accurate.

My business is uncovering the ugliness in people's lives and telling them the truth they so desperately need. I've learned that telling people the truth is a beautiful act of love. Jesus came with grace and truth (John 1:14); He told us the truth about God and about ourselves so that we would have the chance to repent and turn to Him in order to be saved for eternity. When God drew me to Him, and I acknowledged the ugly truth about myself and the choices I had made, He saved me from my sins and then healed me from the inside out. I no longer live under the weight of a guilty conscience, and I'm not trapped by the shame from my past.

Because of God's love, I no longer live behind the self-made prison bars of a pretext.

CHAPTER 2
THE POWER OF FORGIVENESS

"There is therefore now no condemnation for those who are in Christ Jesus. For the law of the Spirit of life has set you free in Christ Jesus from the law of sin and death."
—Romans 8:1-2

Over the years following my conversion, I grew as a Christian, and I felt God leading me to minister to others, especially through my work as a PI. Though I was eager to talk to friends about Jesus and what He had done in my life, I felt deep compassion toward the offenders I worked with. As the anger I had felt since childhood drained out of me, a love for others, especially offenders and other angry young men, was replacing it.

Like a lot of men and women in prison who were abused, my father's cruelty had been the fuel tank for so much of my rage. From Sunday school lessons at my mom's church when I was growing up, I knew that children were supposed to obey their parents (Ephesians 6:1), but I spent the better part of my childhood hiding from my father. The slam of his car door was one of the most terrifying sounds, because it signaled his arrival home from work and the likelihood that I'd be hit, shoved, or yelled at without warning. It wasn't until I was in my mid-forties that I heard the rest of that passage in Ephesians: "Fathers, do not provoke your children to anger, but bring them up in the discipline and instruction of the Lord" (6:4). The word translated "provoke" literally means "to anger alongside" in the original Greek language. It means to exasperate or enrage. As a kid, I didn't realize that instead of training me in God's ways, my father was training me how to be angry alongside him through his ongoing pattern of abuse. In fact, the only time I asked my dad why he didn't go to church with me and my mom, he drove me into the floor with his fist until I was flat on my back. With his hand pressed hard against my mouth, he told me he had been to church all his life, and he knew the Bible.

In that moment, I was terrified. All my life, I knew my father scared me, but I didn't know that he was also inadvertently training me to be exasperated and enraged—like father, like son.

Unfortunately, he didn't just hit me with his hands: he hit me with his words, too. Adults can trounce children with horrible labels and mocking, sarcastic put-downs. The Bible says that rash words pierce our hearts like sword thrusts (Proverbs 12:18), and my dad repeatedly stabbed me with nasty, pitiless insults and name-calling. Interestingly, Paul also wrote the same command about not provoking children to the fathers in the Colossian church, but he added one important detail: he told those fathers that such abusive treatment would make their children discouraged, disheartened, or broken in spirit (Colossians 3:21). After enduring my dad's physical, verbal, and emotional abuse for years, I was definitely broken in spirit and covering that pain with the fury I had learned from him.

With the amount of rage that was in my heart and the ways that I acted on it, I am amazed that I never went to prison. I was shame-filled, hostile, profane in my words, and frequently intoxicated. I drank too much, too often to numb the pain. Though I had never hurt anyone physically, and I hadn't committed felonies to support an addiction, I wasn't sure the word "never" would be true forever. I had the same shame and the same dysfunction as the criminals I was working with, and I didn't have God or a vision of a healthy, forgiven future in Him. I was an exasperated, disheartened kid in a grown man's body—deadening the feelings of rejection and worthlessness with booze and cigarettes, not God's grace.

When I read those verses about how fathers were to treat their children, I realized that God never wanted my father to treat me like that. My dad had ignored God's command to love me. Even more than that, I found that God Himself was a loving Father—compassionate, kind, and slow to anger (Psalm 103:8). I can trust Him and He lifts me up when I'm down, instead of kicking me (Psalm 145:14). I can approach God in prayer and He listens to me instead of ignoring me (1 John 5:14). God even invites us to call Him Abba or "Daddy" (Romans 8:15). I never called my father "Daddy." I never felt close enough or safe enough to call him that. My father was abrasive and hard-hearted toward me and toward people in general, but as I read the Bible, I saw Jesus' tenderheartedness toward people—how he was willing to connect deeply with others and cry for those he loved (John 11:35; Luke 19:41). As I learned more about God through His Word and felt more of His Spirit, I realized this was the kind of Father I wanted.

And this was the kind of father I wanted to be.

Because the anger had melted from my heart and I dropped my pretexts, I truly had to rely on God instead of a tough exterior to protect me in risky, uncertain situations. At first, this was scary. It took time to come to believe that God never fails, that He will always have my back and guide my footsteps. I was also able to see that many other men were just like me. In many cases, I was able to research and ask questions about the offender's life until I saw some close similarities. Empathy became a strong quality for my success. It was something that many other people working in the criminal justice system didn't have. However, empathy doesn't mean I condone what the criminal has done. If I stand before victims and juries and neutralize or minimize criminal behavior, I will soon find myself unemployed. Unfortunately, law enforcement professionals often grandstand and condemn criminals, making speeches about the evil, vileness, and "worthless human waste standing in the courtroom today."

Most people don't look at a criminal and think, "Yeah, that could have been me." Unfortunately, most of the time we can be like the Pharisee in Jesus' parable about the repentant tax collector: we see criminals and inwardly, self-righteously thank God we're not them (Luke 18:11). We miss the point that we all once lived for our own desires and not God's desires; we all sinned; we all needed a Savior (Ephesians 2:1-10). I have yet to meet anyone who gets saved and is suddenly and entirely without a struggle. We grow in grace, and character transformation is a process (2 Peter 1:5-8; 3:18).

This is one of the most important lessons of my stories: To walk with God doesn't mean you have to be a perfect person. God saves imperfect people who recognize their imperfections, humble themselves, repent, and confess that Jesus is Lord (Romans 10:9). Like the tax collector in Jesus' parable (Luke 18:9-14), we ask God to have mercy on us and, in His great love and compassion, He saves us.

I believe that in the process of the tax collector's repentance in Jesus' parable, he felt a lot of shame. Both criminal offenders and their families also experience shame. Though we sometimes use the words shame and embarrassment interchangeably, they're not the same thing. I think of embarrassment as the uncomfortable emotion we experience when we've done something dumb: we said the wrong thing at the wrong time; we tripped over our own two feet; we farted in public. When we're embarrassed, we get red-faced and stammer, but we can often laugh it off and make a joke of our gaffes.

Not so with shame. Shame is a debilitating, cripplingly painful emotion that tells us we are completely worthless. It washes over us and through us, tells us we're unlovable and no good, and causes us to hide the source of our shame from others. Our deep parts become walled off, isolated. Shame and secrecy go hand-in-hand—when I think of a facial expression associated with shame, I can't see it, because in my mind, the offenders' faces are always hidden in their hands. This is why I think the tax collector was experiencing shame: he was standing away from the others in the story, and he could barely raise his eyes to look up to God. He understood that he had fallen short of God's law and that he deserved God's punishment (Romans 3:23).

A lot of criminal offenders experience shame in relation to falling short of man's law, especially if their crimes have harmed others. But if an offender experiences shame, or deep humiliation and a guilty conscience for harming others, but not Godly sorrow—a grief over his sin because his sin was against God, and he does not want to grieve God or be at odds with God anymore—then he can become stuck in shame, or what the Bible calls "worldly sorrow," which won't lead to salvation (2 Corinthians 7:10).

Instead of leading to salvation, this shame, or worldly sorrow, can breed resentment, isolation, and inappropriate hostility toward others. Shame is a close cousin to rage.

Several years ago, I met a young guy named Greg who was deeply humiliated after being sucker punched by a bully on a grade school playground. Since that incident, he vowed that he would never be someone's punching bag: he would always strike first. By the time he told me that story, he had kept that vow for almost twenty years.

When Greg was saved, he worshipped, prayed, read the Bible, and made what his friends described as an unbelievable turnaround in his life; however, in matters of conflict, his penchant for throwing the first punch never left him. As a young husband, he was aggressive whenever he felt defensive, and his aggression was quickly escalating toward domestic abuse. Shame and embarrassment were ruling his actions rather than love. Fearing for her safety, his new bride moved back to her parents' home. He had not physically harmed her, and she hoped for a chance to save their marriage through counseling and the Word of God rather than the criminal justice system.

After a few weeks of tension, Greg accepted an invitation to meet for some individual counseling, and this was when the brokenness in his heart was identified. He had spent a lot of time on the streets as a kid. After the humiliating scene with the playground bully, violence became a normal way of life for him. As a young adult, he recognized that his aggression would soon lead to prison, so he entered the military, where he excelled as an infantryman but returned from war with PTSD.

Greg's "hit first, ask questions later" credo from childhood haunted his military experience. In Iraq, he was part of a perimeter detail for a special operations team. On one particular mission, he guarded a ravine trail while the team went ahead and attacked insurgents. His job was to engage any insurgents who might approach the team from the rear. For nearly 24 hours he listened to the wind interrupted by the occasional distant echoes of a fire fight. On the hill over the ravine, he could see that a woman with some children looked him over with curiosity. He moved into a different position and was observed by a man walking with some camels. Alone, with orders to wait for his team's return, he faced a dilemma: wait or strike first. Rules of war said not to target civilians, but in the countryside, civilians and enemies were a very confusing mix. His obedience to wait for his team, who returned without losses, was conflicted with decisions on how to handle observers who could have reported his position, leading to the death or capture of the entire team. It was situations like this that triggered Greg's "strike first" approach, and the 24 hours during which he didn't strike out were mentally terrifying and torturous to him. He felt powerless and alone.

This brief story is not about the ethics of war or PTSD, but about those life experiences that lead a man or woman to be whom they are. Greg's deep desire to avoid shame and humiliation, rooted in early childhood, led to a life of striking others first rather than turning the other cheek. It wasn't until Greg and his wife sought pastoral counseling together that these deep-seated issues were exposed to the light of grace and given a chance to heal. Thankfully, he was willing to admit how avoiding shame had driven his actions. He repented of those actions and changed his ways.

A significant element of Greg's repentance was his willingness to forgive the people who had hurt him when he was younger, including the playground bully and the people on the streets he had fought. This did not mean that he visited each one of them individually. He did not seek out the playground bully, ring his doorbell, and say "I forgive you!" There is a difference between forgiveness and reconciliation. Some people are not safe to reconcile with; some people are no longer around to reconcile with. Though it is not always possible to reconcile, it is always possible to forgive.

When we are born again, God's Spirit regenerates our hearts so that we can live out the principles in His Word, including forgiving others and even loving our enemies (Matthew 5:44). The work of God's Spirit in our hearts enables us to love people who have harmed us. Only Jesus had the grace to come to earth for the express purpose of dying for us when we were his enemies (Romans 5:8; Colossians 1:21-22). When we respond to His grace, He infuses us with that same extravagant love so we can love our enemies as well as our brothers and sisters in Christ. It is this kind of love that tells the world we are truly followers of Jesus (John 13:35).

In my experience, forgiving others includes two things: emotionally grieving the pain that was caused (in Greg's case, the shame and humiliation), and then consciously giving up the right to hold a grudge or get even with the person who caused the pain. And we forgive not so we can feel better, but because Jesus said we cannot be forgiven for our sins unless we forgive others (Mark 11:26). If I think about how much my sin grieved God, and how much He has forgiven me, then it is hard not to forgive others for the pain they have caused me.

Additionally, when a person exposes their pain to the grace of God and to other people who care and empathize, it helps the person to feel loved and less alone. Because Greg was willing to repent of the harm he was causing others—especially his wife—share his hurts, and forgive those who had hurt him, God healed his festering emotional wounds, and this couple was eventually able to reunite.

I wish I could say the rest of the men in this book were able to avoid prison. Unfortunately, it often takes a person coming face-to-face with the legal consequences of a crime to turn him toward God. Like Greg, though, every man accused or convicted of a crime has some life scars. They may be physical, emotional, psychological, or some combination, but they are there. The shame and pain associated with these scars can warp a person's thinking so much that he becomes detached from reality and does things he would never have done in his right mind. Social isolation, child abuse, grief, fear, rejection, poverty, drug addiction, divorce, alcohol, parental alienation, violence—these are just some of the experiences that afflict people, cause shame, and fuel their decisions to commit crime. If we have empathy and openheartedness to understand the scars that lead the least of our brothers and sisters into prison, and we minister to them with the truth of God's Word, then perhaps we can help them to believe God can save them.

Our forgiveness is critical, because the criminal justice system is not designed for such empathy toward convicts. Since my work as a PI focuses primarily on criminal defense cases, I have attended more sentencing hearings than I can count. These are the court proceedings where the victim tells the judge how the crime has made an impact on his or her life. The victim often cries and shouts at the defendant as he or she lets loose every sad, angry, hurt feeling experienced during the trauma of the crime and the trial. They have every right to do this, and I understand the tremendous emotion they must feel at being victimized. Then too many district attorneys talk indirectly about the offender as a worthless, flawed, and stupid piece of human waste. After this, the DA asks the judge to protect society from evil via a long, harsh prison sentence. While I do not intend to downplay the harm done to a victim or a victim's family, I do want to illustrate the enormous shame that is frequently heaped upon the defendant during this proceeding.

And what does the criminal say in response? He usually unfolds a dirty scrap of paper pulled from his front shirt pocket, and reads a handprinted paragraph that usually sounds something like, "Judge, I'm sorry to the people I hurt, and I want to thank my public defender, and tell my mom I love her."

Like the tax collector, the defendant's eyes usually never leave the paper to look up at the judge or the victim.

Sometimes the judge finishes the hearing with another big verbal barrage of ridicule, while other judges merely make a little speech affirming the words of the victim… and then off everyone goes, and the criminal is handcuffed and disappears for a long time.

Sentencing is a very painful process to watch. When a victim is in pain, sobbing, angry, and broken, it is heart-wrenching. When a defendant is remorseful and openly crying from regret, guilt, shame, and the fear of going to prison, it is also agonizing. I'm at the point where it is a struggle to attend these hearings and watch a man be handcuffed and taken through the door, which eventually leads to prison.

Additionally, the anger and tears of the family members who occasionally witness a sentencing hearing are also hard to see—both the victims' families and the defendants' families. In particular, the defendants' families, who are stigmatized by association, also experience profound shame from the time a defendant is charged to the time he is convicted, and then throughout the duration of his time behind bars, and even when he is paroled. There is a deep social stigma associated with being a convict or the family member of a convict, and even once the man is freed from prison, his status as a free man is tainted with the label "ex-con." This affects his family, as well.

After one sentencing hearing, I remember a very awkward elevator ride with two women, both of whom I knew well. One was my client, Marcia. She was professionally dressed and in court to see the sentencing of a young heroin dealer who had been giving dope to her daughter and then allowing his crew to sexually assault her while she was high. Many of these encounters occurred in Marcia's home while she and her husband were out for the evening. Marcia's husband had an extensive gun collection that was also being tapped by the crew, and it wasn't until one of these stolen guns turned up in a street crime that police were led back to him.

Working with the police, Marcia's husband identified that his gun collection had been pilfered and several weapons were missing. Police questioned the daughter, who initially denied knowledge of the theft and lied to cover up her addiction. Police charged her with the theft of the firearms and while in a juvenile detention center, she confessed to what really occurred.

The heroin dealer was sentenced to two to four years in state prison for the theft of the firearms. His mother, Gina, was the other woman in the elevator that day. She wore a leather jacket, black t-shirt, and torn jeans. I had originally met Gina while investigating a crash in which her brother was killed. During that investigation, Gina and I had talked at length about her brother and his backstory of abuse and unhappiness that led to his alcoholism. He was driving drunk when he rolled his pickup truck multiple times on a country highway. Back then, she had talked about her son and how she knew he was messed up with substances, just like her brother. Gina loved her son and he was all that remained of her family. She had been through many relationships since the son was born and said no one wanted a poor woman with a young son. Eventually no relationship could endure an aging woman with a troubled son. She was grief- stricken over the loss of her brother, and now her son was being swallowed by prison.

The women cried as the elevator descended, but they had no idea what I knew. It was not until I had stepped into the elevator that I put the facts and the names together. Gina's son had victimized Marcia's family. I felt bad for both mothers, but I became nervous that there would be a confrontation.

When the elevator doors opened, we stepped out, and the mothers turned to each other. I held my breath, wondering what Marcia would say. As Marcia extended her hand to Gina and introduced herself, Gina broke into loud sobs. The two mothers hugged and cried in the public lobby of the courthouse outside of the elevators. I stood near the main lobby door and waited. Remarkably, they walked out ahead of me, Marcia with her arm over Gina's shoulder, holding her in comfort.

Though Marcia had gotten justice, she still harbored deep fear about leaving her house unprotected after what had happened in its walls. Her daughter was battling an opiate addiction, and the sexual assaults had left the girl infected with hepatitis C. Yet despite all that Gina's son had done, Marcia willingly put her arm around Gina's shoulders because she needed comfort. To my surprise, instead of watching a fight, I got to see how Marcia's friendship and forgiveness began to heal Gina's shame and loss. Unlike the Pharisee, Marcia didn't let Gina stand at a distance from her, unable to make eye contact; instead, she drew her close and comforted her in her pain. At the time, I didn't understand how such forgiveness could bring people out of isolation and allow true healing to begin.

Now that I know how important forgiveness is to God and others, I know that we as Christians need to be careful not to assume the role of the Pharisee, who stands next to the shame-filled tax collector, stares straight into the heavens, and declares his own righteousness. According to Jesus, he was not the one who walked away justified by God.

Just as I've noticed a pattern of shame, unforgiveness, and isolation in the men that I've worked with, you may also see this pattern in the stories in this book. But thankfully, the Bible says that those who believe in Jesus will not be put to shame (Romans 9:33, 10:11). When we turn to Him and He saves us and heals us, He takes away our guilt and shame, and our hearts no longer condemn us (Romans 8:1-2; 1 John 3:21). This is the freedom that is in Christ Jesus, even when a man is behind bars.

CHAPTER 3
MITIGATING CIRCUMSTANCES

"My little children, I am writing these things to you so that you may not sin. But if anyone does sin, we have an advocate with the Father, Jesus Christ the righteous."

—1 John 2:1

W hen an accused offender admits his or her criminal acts before a court, this admission is known as a plea. It is officially expressed as "the defendant pleads guilty." Guilt is also determined by the unanimous decision of a jury. Twelve fair and impartial citizens have heard the evidence that supports the accusations, and, after considering evidence and testimony in the offender's defense, the jurors all agree to a guilty verdict. After guilt is admitted or decided by a jury, the case moves into the phase where punishment is calculated. The punishment, or consequence for committing the crime, is referred to as a sentence. Sentences are determined by legal guidelines that categorize crimes based on their seriousness and their impact on the victim and society.

Sentencing also takes into consideration the offender's prior record. A first-time offender will receive a lesser sentence than a repeat offender.

While my work as a PI relates to all stages of the criminal proceedings, a significant part of my investigative work involves the preparation of forensic social history reports for the defense attorney to use in court at the time of sentencing. These reports are popularly nicknamed mitigation reports, or, as I call them, mitigation profiles. These profiles are designed to do exactly what the name implies—mitigate or reduce the prison sentence due to the circumstances in the offender's life that led him to commit the crime.

Some believe mitigation is a gimmick in which the attorney attempts to offer information to dilute the seriousness of the crime. The most challenging negative comments I hear about mitigation profiles include people who say they are "just an attempt to deflect blame." Usually this perspective is supported with statements like, "Lots of people have hard lives, but not everyone becomes a criminal." The purpose of a mitigation profile is not to demonstrate that an offender had a "hard life" or to "deflect blame" onto parents, authority figures, or life circumstances. The purpose of a mitigation profile is to identify an underlying explanation for the crime as well as any rehabilitation needs that could prevent an offender from committing future crimes. An explanation, however, is not an excuse. The offender is ultimately held responsible—the profile simply helps the court to understand why the offender committed the crime and to discern meaningful ways to prevent criminal behavior in the future.

A mitigation profile is a detailed report about the offender's life that includes their achievements as well as their failures. In the criminal justice system, an offender's character and life experiences are flattened out so that the crime he has committed becomes the sum total of his identity. The crime becomes his master status, or how he is known in society. In order to win a case and prove the defendant's guilt, the prosecuting attorneys, police officers, and victims emphasize the vile nature not just of the crime, but of the offender himself. In the courtroom, I've watched this descend into ruthless name-calling and condemnation:

"Worthless human being."

"Human garbage."

"Living trash."

"Demonic."

"A mistake of life."

"A waste of the air we breathe."

When I write a profile, I attempt to offer a fuller perspective of the offender as a human being beyond the flat perspectives these epithets depict.

I begin a profile by introducing a problem or conflict involving the offender, and then I tell the story about how it gets worse for him. The story could be the offender's version of the crime. That version often includes a lot of confession and remorse. If the offender is not willing to admit and openly disclose what occurred, then I am wasting my time. Receiving mercy from the court in the form of a reduced sentence requires an admission of guilt.

Remorse, however, takes a variety of forms. Some men are highly aware of the pain they caused others, and some men turn their guilt inward, casting self-blame. It isn't uncommon for an offender to use the same destructive, shaming words as the prosecutor:

"I'm a piece of trash."

"I should have been aborted."

"No one ever loved me."

My goal in the mitigation profile is to demonstrate to the judge how this offender came into contact with the victim, and then explain how that contact led to the crime for which the offender is charged. For some men, their crimes were spontaneous, poorly conceived plans born out of anger, jealousy, or lust. For many men, their crimes were an outgrowth of one or more past traumatic event that scarred their identity. Trauma is the most common factor I have seen in the men and women with whom I have worked. For some, their subsequent grief and substance abuse are closely entwined with their trauma experiences.

I've worked with offenders who've experienced many forms of trauma—child sexual abuse, war-related PTSD, unresolved grief over the death of a loved one, bullying, humiliation by teachers, domestic violence, divorce and relationship problems, and criminal victimization are some examples. What may merely inconvenience or temporarily anger one man might cause a deep painful memory to another man. Some people ruminate for an evening while others dwell on traumatic memories for decades. People change. The brain changes and that change can become immediate and profound. Ultimately, trauma causes us to look inward, and when we are looking at ourselves, we are the sole focus. Often, because we are traumatized, our attention is focused on healing or, at the very least, protecting our wounds, and not on care and concern for others. For many of the offenders I've worked with, past traumatic experiences have caused them to become very self-focused and self-protective.

A further purpose of the mitigation profile is to present the positive characteristics and achievements in the offender's life story. I introduce family members, role models, mentors, and the dreams and aspirations the offender may have. I discuss their academic, athletic, artistic, or vocational achievements. This is balanced with the "warts and all" composite sketch that does not candy coat the offender's poor life choices or deceive anyone in the court into dismissing the facts. The mitigation profile does not lose sight of the fact that the offender committed a crime and hurt someone, sometimes many people.

To write a mitigation profile, I interview defendants and people relevant to a case in order to drill down to the root causes of why the defendant committed a crime. During these interviews, I attempt to discover the offender's motivation. The crime is the bad fruit, and the motivation is the bad root. I'm interested in what is happening in the defendant's heart as a result of his past experiences and relationships. Every criminal I meet has had some form of suffering. You could say they were imprisoned in life before they were locked up physically. After conducting numerous interviews for these profiles, I've observed a pattern of three elements that are present in the stories of the vast majority of offenders I've worked with: painful past experiences, often in early childhood, that caused deep, abiding shame; unforgiveness toward those who caused the pain; and social isolation intended to hide the pain. The offenders may have friends, sometimes they're the life of the party, but the shameful past is kept carefully isolated and hidden from view.

Because my profiles demand that I dig around in the offender's past, and because the offender is motivated to reduce his prison sentence or avoid being locked up altogether, I am usually the first person to whom he is willing to tell his pain-filled story. When I discuss the offender's past experiences with family members during secondary interviews, they are often shocked to learn about them, because they had been well hidden for so long. The only evidence of their existence was the bad fruit in the offender's life: the substance abuse, the acting out, the petty crimes and misdemeanors, the emotional instability, the lack of responsibility, or the like. Sometimes the bad fruit doesn't ripen until it's given the right environment, such as the freedom of living away from home at college.

Also unique to my position as a PI, though I ask these offenders a lot of questions about their experiences, I don't condemn them for their crime. I just collect the facts to write their stories for the purpose of mitigating their charges and, if applicable, reducing their prison sentences. Because I have expertise in the justice system and criminal psychology, I don't judge. Because I'm on their side, they feel comfortable sharing their stories. In addition, their crimes have not injured me, nor would I be personally wounded if they share their secrets. Thus, for many offenders, I become the ideal confidant.

By interviewing offenders at such a deep emotional level, I've unlocked a door into the faith and beliefs that offenders have regarding God. My own love for God, coupled with a gritty, blunt attitude, has enabled me to talk about faith and share the truth of Jesus with many offenders. Just recently, I asked a young guy accused of sexual assault if he wanted to pray together. He nodded and asked how I knew he wanted to pray. He had been praying his rosary the entire day. Often these guys are looking for God because they know everyone and everything else has failed them. Other times, these offenders look at God the Father as if He were no more reliable than the earthly father who abandoned or abused him. Not everyone is open or welcoming to God's healing. And not everyone is willing to let down his guard enough to become vulnerable. We all need to break before we can be fixed, and some of these guys are guarding their shame so carefully, they're not willing to break.

Though I've learned through my own experiences with shame, pain, unforgiveness, and isolation that healing is possible, I don't have a pie-in-the-sky view that every offender will experience this, because some are unwilling to open their hearts to God's love and healing. I do know, however, that God extends amazing grace toward people who have committed crimes, even very heinous crimes, and their hearts can melt under the warmth of God's love.

People, including judges and prosecutors, like stories better than arguments. A truthful story in a mitigation profile can help victims understand why they suffered at the hands of their offender. This, coupled with a sincere, humble apology, may help the victim to find closure more easily, especially if the profile enables the victim to avoid testifying in court. It's easy for some professionals to forget about the victim when a criminal case goes into the court system. A police officer is concerned about evidence, and a prosecutor is concerned about winning a conviction. The defense attorney or public defender may be concerned about the defendant's rights and jail time, and the offender is often focused on himself and his fate. But for there to be justice, there must be some fairness that begins to restore the victim to normalcy. Maybe no one can be brought back from death or from serious bodily injury, but the consequence of prison is all that society has to offer in return. I very strongly believe that by offering a victim an objective truthful story that highlights the offender's trauma, life course, and remorse for his crime, that I have done more to help restore a victim than any prosecutor could through name-calling and humiliation of the offender in the public court.

The mitigation profile usually results in a successful and agreeable plea bargain that includes a reduction in charges or a reduction in the prison sentence, or sometimes both, coupled with additional rehabilitation recommendations that can benefit the offender further in life. My job is not about getting someone off charges or keeping someone out of jail. I see my job more powerfully as helping the defense attorney to understand the offender and make sure the offender does the right time for the right charges. This is usually a very complex process.

Thankfully, I had a slight preview of writing such profiles when I wrote social history reports during my past law enforcement experience as a county probation officer. An important part of my duties as a probation officer was writing pre-sentence investigation reports (PSIs) for the court judge to read prior to sentencing an offender to jail time. My reports followed a standard format with narrative details ranging from one or two sentences to a few paragraphs. The PSI was a tight document, much shorter and simpler than a mitigation profile, but it was well investigated. I verified the information provided by the offender and even spoke with family or employers. I regularly obtained school records.

Like a mitigation profile, the PSI included the offender's version of the incident, and it was often this portion that required more words to detail the "offender, victim, crime scene" connection. Most people think "means, motive, opportunity" when explaining the crime, but I have rarely met an offender who could explain it that eloquently. Most of the time, the offender would color his version of the story with neutralizing statements and excuses that diluted his responsibility or minimized the damage and harm to the victim. I ended the PSI with an evaluative memo to the judge. This was written as a separate page at the very end of the report and was designed to be torn loose from the rest of the document and studied closely by the judge.

If someone lied to me, I would include that deception in the report. If they cried, if they mocked the victim, if they expressed regret, if they were delusional with mental illness, I would include those observations. I wrote a PSI for every offender who was going to be sentenced to prison. In my short career as a probation officer, I wrote a lot of PSIs. In each, I couldn't help but include those mitigating factors and small stories of suffering that helped to accentuate the offender's humanity. I was surprised to learn how much credibility some judges placed in my opinion of the criminal offender, as written in the evaluative summary memo.

There are two fundamental problems with a PSI, however. First, it is a standardized, formatted report, which leaves little room to individualize the information based on the case and the offender. Second, it is written solely from a law enforcement perspective. A probation officer is law enforcement, and most probation officers have not had formal training in social work or an education in trauma. Based on this, the PSI has limitations that the mitigation report does not.

After beginning my relationship with God, I recognized the extent of the trauma I had suffered at the hands of my father. Over time, God healed those wounds and transformed my character, and along with it, my identity. I am no longer the same person I was ten years ago. But this transformation has not made me spiritually haughty; if anything, my relationship with God has helped me to see how weak I am on my own, and how reliant I am on Him for everything. Because of my walk with God, and because of my own sins and scars, I see a little of myself in the offenders I meet now. I have a deeper understanding for the destruction that unhealed trauma can bring to a person's life.

When I interview offenders for mitigation profiles, I often get the discernment needed to ask painful, pointed questions to uncover that trauma, by the Holy Spirit's leading. I seek to understand the pretexts that offenders use to mask their real, wounded identities, and then work, by God's guidance, to uncover those real identities and include them in the mitigation profile. God has given me that ability to be deeper in my objectivity, and He has given me that boldness to write bluntly or with emotion, depending on what needs to be communicated. But most of all God has given me a heart to help the offender, and the victim, to gain understanding. This is the opportunity for both to heal.

CHAPTER 4

PRISON IS HELL

"I am the door. If anyone enters by me, he will be saved and will go in and out and find pasture."
—John 10:9

Because I have worked for decades in and around the prison system, I know the benefit of reducing a prison sentence for an offender, if this is possible. People often joke about prisons in the U.S. being soft on prisoners, like "country clubs" for white-collar crime, but even the best prisons are little more than depressing, cinderblock tombs for those serving life sentences. The vast majority of prisons, however, are just plain hell.

And unforgiving. That's my strongest memory of the old county jail in my hometown, the first jail I had ever been in.

That fortress of a jail towered above the street, its recessed windows striped with thick vertical bars. The jail was so wide and imposing that the building itself seemed to roll up its sleeves and bully the punier row houses nearby. Two massive bastions, like hulking arms, bordered the portico that lay several steps above the sidewalk. The portico led to the jail's front door, an enormous, thick slab of wood trimmed and reinforced with steel braces. It had an exaggerated brass keyhole on both sides that matched the oversized, tarnished brass key that hung from a heavy chain on the lieutenant's belt. There was only one key—only one way to freedom, out that door—and that key literally never left his side. Back then, at the beginning of my career, I could understand prisoners wanting to escape from that prison, but for the life of me, I had no idea who would want to use the keyhole on the front of the door to enter it.

Inside that jail, it was hell.

A sticky filth covered everything like the floor of a movie theater. No matter how clean a surface may have looked, it felt dirty, polluted. In winter, the air hung hot and wet, like a mingling of shower room and kitchen grease. The moisture would settle on the battleship-gray concrete floor in the cellblocks and make the only cold surface in the place slippery and dangerous. For the prisoners, it was part sauna, part skating rink. In summer, the jail stank of locker room and stale coffee. A box fan laced with brown dust hummed as it blew dead flies around that concrete floor. Everyone sweated.

A curving, narrow stairway echoed people's footsteps as it descended from the fluorescent lights and institutional tile of the intake area toward the crude, cut stone of the foundation below. That stairway led to a long, seemingly never-ending hallway flanked by dark rooms. It was always warm in that hallway, despite the draft that would flow through the cellblocks upstairs. A glowing heat radiated from the furnace room somewhere deeper in the dungeon, and summer intensified the moldiness and humidity in those unlit, cavernous rooms.

I had my first run-in with cockroaches in this jail, and it busted the myth that they were shy, nocturnal insects. They were brown, greasy-looking, as big as baby mice, and everywhere. They fed on the filth of their environment, which unfortunately extended to the prisoners' hygiene. My first experiences in this prison predated orange jumpsuits and striped prisoner uniforms. Inmates wore street clothes, usually the same outfit every day, week after week. Laundry was optional, and some guys chose to spend their money on cigarettes and phone calls instead of detergent or soap. The bitter nose-cocktail of cigarette smoke, body odor, feces, and sickness clung so tightly to the inside of my sinuses that it flavored the drainage in my throat caused by the mold and mildew. I would cough it up, even days after leaving. The air in the jail was so sour and dank, I could understand how people hundreds of years ago believed that diseases were spread by bad air.

And there was disease. Suffering came in the form of tuberculosis, scabies, and ailments from lifelong substance abuse. Hepatitis B and C were rampant, and there was no boundary to the ways prisoners could become infected. I knew a young guy who came in for a DWI arrest. That's driving while intoxicated. Another inmate offered him some chewing tobacco. The two talked for a bit, and while the young guy's head was spinning from the nicotine rush, the other guy spat a stream of tobacco juice into the trash can and then pulled out the wad of chewing tobacco from his own mouth, put it back in the wax-coated cardboard snuff can, stirred it with his finger, and closed the lid. The young guy gagged and then threw up.

It was hell.

Throughout the Gospels, Jesus talked about hell quite a lot. In fact, no one in the Bible spoke more about hell than Jesus did, not even the fieriest of prophets, apostles, or teachers. When I began to read what Jesus said about hell, I thought about this jail and all the prisons that I've visited. Jesus said that hell was a fiery furnace where there will be weeping and gnashing of teeth (Matthew 13:41-42); He said the fire will be unquenchable (Mark 9:43) and the punishment will be eternal

(Matthew 25:46); He said hell will be torment for the people there (Luke 16:23).

Hell is the ultimate life sentence: excruciatingly painful and forever outside the presence of God (2 Thessalonians 1:9). When we are stubborn and not willing to repent, we are actually storing up God's wrath against us (Romans 2:5). Hell is the consequence of God's wrath that Jesus saved us from when he died on the cross and we obey the gospel (Romans 5:8-9).

But I don't believe God threatens us with hell: he warns us of it, the way a responsible father would warn his children not to do something that would cause injury. And hell is not abuse. I've lived through abuse brought on by rage, hatred, selfishness, and resentment. God is not abusive, but He is not permissive, either. Our heavenly Father is holy, righteous, and just, and He tells us that no lawless or disobedient person is going to live in heaven with Him (Revelation 21:8). I hate talking about hell, but if we don't acknowledge that hell exists, it's like walking up to the edge of the Grand Canyon and pretending there is no cliff to fall over. If we don't acknowledge hell as an eternal consequence of God's wrath for unrepented sin, how can we ever truly understand and appreciate God's mercy? If an offender goes into court and pleads not guilty, how does the judge extend mercy? He can't.

Admittedly, though, I try to block hell from my mind. It's painful to think of people who don't know Jesus going there for eternity. It's heavy, even depressing, and I don't like to think about it, anymore than I like going into prisons. For me, prisons are one of the closest approximations of hell on earth. They are a preview of an afterlife without God. Every space is designed to confine and control; the worst punishments are meant to isolate and cause pain.

For example, between the intake administration offices and the cellblocks, there was a small, square space much like a steel trap. In bigger institutions, this space is called a sally port, but in this jail, it was simply called "between the doors." You entered through a heavy steel door, which was locked and unlocked by a guard in the intake area. When someone needed to move from "between the doors," he would pound on the door to get the guard's attention. Pounding on the doors could be a signal, a request, or a statement, depending on what side you were on. Pounding on the doors was also a way to alleviate the tension you felt being trapped "between the doors." When you were in that space, you didn't need to be a convict to feel like a prisoner.

On the other side of this space was another large door of vertical iron bars that opened into the cellblocks. The cells were small rectangles that inmates entered through a low door, much like the doorways of battleships. Inside each cell was a bunk bed with two thin mattresses covered in blue pinstripes. Sometimes there would even be a third mattress on the floor, depending on how full the jail was. Each cell had a stainless steel toilet and a sink that was no bigger than the spittoon at a dentist's office. During the day, the inmates were allowed out of their cells to socialize, play cards, read, or smoke at the tables that ran down the center of the block. For any inmate on isolation or cell restriction, however, their cell stayed locked while other inmates freely passed by and enjoyed these activities.

Seeing the other inmates' freedom to move around was part of the punishment of cell restriction. It fostered competition, resentment, and retribution among the inmates, especially if a "free" inmate lorded his freedom over a restricted one.

Not surprisingly, everyone had a glare of suspicion in that jail. Inmates fought with guards; new commits fought with arresting officers. These weren't mere punches thrown in wild desperation, but true painful suffocating piles of men overtaking the anger or the desperation of someone who just wanted to go home or who couldn't stand the trauma of being shackled or caged. A police officer broke a drunken man's wrists while he was in handcuffs. Once, when a new commit flailed and kicked, a stream of officers flowed into the intake room where they pinned the man down, multiple officers pressing each limb into the floor, until someone with medical credentials tranquilized him. I watched as the sedative melted his violent behavior into heavy, rhythmic breathing. The officers then hogtied him and took him to isolation.

Another time, two inmates on a cleaning detail hatched a plan to take a staff member hostage and use him as a human shield to barge out the front door. One of these inmates picked up a toaster from the staff break room and struck a lieutenant in the back of the head. Disoriented, the lieutenant turned around and grabbed the guy and his partner in a bear hug before falling on them. He was a large man, and his body weight pinned them to the floor until another officer, who had heard the crash, responded. The inmates were traumatized by the incident, and a nurse was called to check them for injuries. The lieutenant got a few days off and an award for stopping a breakout.

As dark as this all felt, the lights in the cell block were always on. The inmates had one television at the end of the block, and this either blared or flickered in silence depending on the mood of the guard on duty. Sometimes an inmate would grab the remote control and change the channel. Another inmate would wrestle it away, and the two would fight until tired or bloody. When this happened, the guards would break things up, often at their own peril. On one occasion, an inmate kicked a guard who had ordered that the TV be turned off. It took several officers to carry the inmate out of the block and into an isolation cell. Because the guard was injured, that inmate was prosecuted and eventually transported to a state prison.

Usually, there were only one or two guards on duty; at night, only the trustees—older inmates who had proven to be cooperative and not dangerous—did most of the block maintenance and were allowed to roam in and out of their cells. Everyone else was locked in after 10 p.m., but it was seldom quiet. Somebody might randomly scream a string of expletives; another might make whooping and animal sounds; others would bang metal cups, shoes, or fists against the bars. These sounds were so loud, they could sometimes be heard all the way into the intake area. Sometimes these sounds were made out of inmates' resentment toward the trustees, who were seen as snitches. Sometimes shouting matches occurred because prisoners were safely tucked away in their cells, and their taunts were anonymous and wouldn't result in brawls. Such scorn was most often reserved for the most vulnerable of inmates.

Obviously, God's law did not reign in that jail. Sure, there were chapel services and Bible studies, but like most jails, religious meetings were an opportunity for inmates to get out of the cell block and mingle with others; such meetings were a chance for prisoners to gossip, complain, and pass messages or cigarettes. Some men would pick up on a Bible verse or act interested in God until after they got parole. Some inmates would try to coerce the pastor into a letter of reference to use at sentencing. Guards and police officers often snidely remarked that when an inmate found God in jail, the bigger the cross hanging around his neck, the guiltier he was.

I used to joke that the only places in town where I felt welcome were the police station and the jail. I've been in a lot of prisons since then, and though I am always vigilant, the fear has diminished over time. That old county jail was remodeled about fifteen years ago and is unrecognizable from its original design. That bully of a building is now much kinder and gentler on the inside. The front door, two frosted glass panels, now sports a regular-sized key cylinder. The lobby has a few rows of vinyl seats and a metal detector for visitors to pass through before proceeding into a short hallway with glass visitation booths. Conversations are conducted over a phone system, and every word is recorded for evidence that could be used against them in a court of law. Ironically, at the right angle in the visitor's booth farthest to the right, inmates can see beyond the visitation area, through the front doors onto the street. But life outside those doors is out of reach, no matter how clear and transparent the portal. As in the parable of the rich man and Lazarus, the rich man in hell could see paradise, but there was a great chasm keeping him from being there (Luke 16:19-31).

The sally port, formerly known as "between the doors," has been transformed into a garage the size of a gymnasium. Police cars pull through like a fast-food restaurant, dropping off drunks or fugitives. Everyone enters through a classification area known as "central" or "booking." Offenders are placed into large cells depending on their condition. There is a drunk tank, some isolation cells, and even a glass enclosure for suicide observation. Beyond this area are the new cellblocks, which are pods of cells or dormitory-style housing, depending on the security level. Everyone wears orange suits, slippers with no soles, and white t-shirts provided by the prison. A full-time nurse and counselor work to administer the buffet of anti-psychotics and narcotic maintenance meds. Inmates are either quietly self-confined on their bunks, or they are standing, hollering through the occasional open door, and making animal sounds to heckle rivals in other blocks.

Another interesting addition to this updated prison is the women. In some areas, they are visible and separated by a glass window. The genders play to one another, flirting sexually. There is clear hatred in these interactions, along with lust and an edge of rape restrained by inches of heavy glass. And there is no privacy accorded to inmates based on gender. Male and female corrections officers walk freely among the population. If a male CO likes to watch a female inmate use the toilet, he will watch her. A female CO may patrol the men's shower. It is part of the duty, part of the punishment. In these instances, shaming the inmates is part of the titillating perks that some members of the prison profession seem to enjoy.

In addition to the free-roaming guards, there are cameras everywhere. Cameras are necessary in most prisons now and have taken the place of some jobs formerly accomplished by guards. The large brass lieutenant's key has been replaced by an electronic lock and a white plastic push button. Instead of opening a door, there is always a harsh voice on a faceless intercom asking for your identity or challenging your reason to pass from one door through the next. Some doors clank locked and unlocked. Some slide open very slowly, like an old elevator. When a door is closed, it doesn't slam anymore with that stereotypic echoing clang of metal, but whoever closes it then hangs on the handle and rocks it back and forth loudly, thump-thump, just to make sure it's really closed.

Even though the jail's rooms and doors are more modern, they're still designed to restrict freedom and eliminate the possibility of escape. One primary rule of this constraint is that only one door opens at a time. For example, in a sally port, one door doesn't open until the door behind it shuts. In society, open doors are a metaphor for freedom and opportunity. In prison, open doors eventually shut and lock. They are secured by alarms and guards with clubs, pepper spray, and high-voltage stun guns. Thus, inmates spend most of their days walking through doors that ultimately go nowhere.

Ironically, most of the prisoners I work with believed that the metaphoric "doors" they walked through to get into prison would lead to freedom. They walked through the door of drug-dealing to make big money, the door of sexual assault to feel powerful, the door of arson to experience sexual arousal (talk to a psychologist about that one), and even the door of murder for revenge. Each man was deceived into believing that his crime would lead to freedom—to peace of mind, to redeemed honor, to a feeling of pleasure, to self worth.

But instead, each crime committed led to a hell on earth: guilt, shame, suffering, disconnection, isolation, loneliness, hopelessness, and powerlessness.

Thinking they had opened the door to freedom, they had actually opened the door to hell, here and in eternity.

Jesus said that He is The Door (John 10:9). When we obey the gospel, He saves us and sets us free. In the word picture He uses to describe Himself as the door to a sheep pen, in which we are His sheep, He says that we will be able to go "in and out." We will no longer be trapped or confined spiritually; we will no longer be spiritually dead in our sins; instead, we'll have salvation in Him. And He will give us "pasture"—He'll feed us and sustain us with His Word and His Spirit.

Even when men and women are behind bars, they can still experience salvation and spiritual freedom in Jesus. No matter how many closed doors they experience in this hell on earth, Jesus remains an Open Door to them. They just need someone to show them the key.

CHAPTER 5
REVENGE

"You have heard that it was said, 'An eye for an eye, and a tooth for a tooth.' But I say to you, Do not resist the one who is evil. But if anyone slaps you on the right cheek, turn to him the other also."
—Matthew 5:38-39

Mark waited at the kitchen table in the empty house and drank a can of soda. The overcast gray of twilight filled the room as he waited. He listened to the occasional sound of cars rolling by, eager to hear the one he was waiting for. He killed time by double-checking that the back door was unlocked and ajar. That door would be his exit strategy when it was all over. He walked around the bedroom looking over some photographs. Poking through the closet, he spied a deer rifle that had been reported stolen many years ago. It was leaning in the corner of the man's closet.

Mark had been blamed for taking that gun. Now he knew who had it.

Before he had gotten to the house, Mark had decided that if he heard the man's children coming through the door with their father, he would immediately flee through that open back door. Mark would not scar this man's children the way this man had scarred his. Mark's plan for revenge was ten years in the making. Another day or week or even year wouldn't matter if it meant shielding those children from harm.

During those ten years, Mark had not been allowed to see his own children, and to him, those years had moved at a glacial speed. He knew he hadn't been a perfect husband, but he believed he had done nothing to deserve being separated from his children. Mark's own father had abandoned him along with his two brothers and two sisters when Mark was about three years old, and this left him feeling confused and deeply rejected. Mark himself had four children, two boys and two girls, and his connection to them was Mark's whole world. He would never have abandoned them, but through a horrible twist of fate, he had lost them. By losing his children, Mark had lost all but two feelings: love for them and hatred for the man who had taken them away, along with his entire life. And hatred won. Tonight hatred would conquer.

Mark sat down again at the kitchen table and waited as the gray sky turned into night. Next to his soda lay a pump shotgun he had stolen from a little cabin in the mountains. He had shortened the barrel with a hack-saw and stolen some shells from that same cabin. While wandering the house, Mark had also found the man's old revolver in a drawer.

The cylinder was loaded.

Around 7 p.m., the jarring grind of the garage door signaled the man's arrival. As the car pulled in, Mark quietly picked up the shotgun and aimed for the door that separated the garage from the kitchen. Would there be children? He heard one car door open and slam shut. A single set of footsteps scuffed toward the door.

He was alone.

As the door opened, Mark fired the first shot and repeated the same words he had said ten years earlier—that he had promised to take the man's last breath from him.

One shot for each year.

When it was over, Mark had used every bullet and shell, including the last one he had originally considered using for himself. He had even used the man's own revolver against him.

No one would ever see this man's face again.

From the day that Mark believed that there was an affair between this man and his wife, Mark had determined to get revenge. Mark's was a dedicated, all-consuming, calculating rage: one that he felt justified to act on.

I met Mark for the first time in an old gymnasium of a county prison. All the meeting rooms, visiting rooms, and attorney-client rooms were full. The only activity not going on was rec, so the basketball court was the only quiet place available. We sat in metal chairs near the foul line and talked uninterrupted for hours.

The court appointed me as the principal investigator assigned to Mark's defense attorney. Mark and I would spend one long year together as I worked on his case to develop the forensic social history profile with the details a jury would need if they were to show mercy for his life.

Originally, I didn't want to become involved with a murderer. Violent homicides are emotionally difficult cases—autopsy photos, photos of the crime scene, the recounting of the crime, the motives of the criminal, and the anguish of the family—these things in past cases had given me nightmares and led to depression. Almost ten years prior, I had worked on a multiple-victim homicide case that had involved a shotgun, something akin to the crime in Capote's *In Cold Blood*. Mark's case was reminiscent of that, except for one thing: I now knew Jesus. As I prayed, I felt deeply impressed by God to take Mark's case—I felt as though I was Mark's last chance to know God, too. God clearly had a purpose for me in Mark's life.

Our meeting on that basketball court started like any other interview. Mark's attorney introduced us. I shook his hand and was impressed that it was un-cuffed despite his charges. I could tell he was stressed as he blew a big exhale through a jutted lower lip. The air breezed up his face and blew the straight black bangs out of his eyes. He smiled without opening his lips and looked sideways at me.

I gave him my verbal resume: Detective license. Violent crimes. Educated. Know the system. Know the streets. Know people. Divorced, too. Father.

What I didn't mention was how much of my old self I saw in him: Imprisoned. Confused. Lonely. Very angry.

Mark unfolded the murder and the ten years of prison and pain since he first confronted the man, accusing him of the affair. Mark had told him, "If you ever come around my wife and family again, I promise I will take your last breath."

When he said this, he had poked the end of a steel pipe into the man's arm.

Within days, Mark had found himself confined in a county correctional facility, and it would be years until he was released on parole for assault with a deadly weapon.

While he was locked up, Mark's wife divorced him.

Upon his release, he went straight to his kids. The courts were unsympathetic to visitation rights for a convicted felon and Mark gave up. He would later confess that he never fought for his kids because he didn't know how. Destitute and heartbroken, Mark reflected that his own father had never fought for him. Though he couldn't quite put it into words, in his mind, a father losing his kids was something that just happened in life. It was not a matter of control or of opportunity. You just lost.

As we talked, Mark insisted that any defense investigation must be generous toward his ex-wife. "She is the mother of my children," he had said. "I don't want anything to cause them to blame their mother."

When Mark told me that he committed this murder for his kids, it was a motive so familiar to me. I knew hatred very well. I knew resentment, bitterness, and grudges. And I knew what it meant to love a child so much that I would do anything if I felt there was a need to protect that child.

To Mark, this man drove a wedge deep into his family. He divided their time from their mother. And he blocked Mark's time with his children, too. Mark was to never call or visit. The children were to abandon Mark's memory. Mark did not exist.

But Mark *did* exist, and in subtle and not-so-subtle ways, he continued to try to see his kids. He'd call the house or show up unexpectedly at ballgames. He knew where they went fishing on summer evenings. He stayed in the shadows of the family among other outcasts and relatives who gossiped and filled his head with jealousy. When the painful, parental alienation became overwhelming, Mark retreated to street life with his brother and cousins, who were heavily dosed with heroin, weed, and alcohol.

Mark was jailed repeatedly for parole violations and new charges. Each time he would be a compliant but unhealed inmate, until he eventually worked the system, did his time, and found himself back on the streets to continue the cycle of desperation and self-destruction. During this time, Mark thought of little else but this man and what he had done to his family. It was this man who had taken Mark's wife and now Mark's children. Mark blamed him utterly for the destruction of his family.

It was also during this time that Mark had met an older woman who lived in another city more than a hundred miles from his children. He moved into her apartment, and they spent idle days together, watching television and smoking cigarettes. Each day they took time to read to each other from a thick King James Bible. That Bible would become a strange exhibit of evidence during the case, and later the object of the most important question I could use to challenge Mark.

Mark's relationship with this woman lasted only a few weeks before he was overcome with emotion for his children. He was falling apart psychologically. One afternoon he borrowed her car and left to buy cigarettes.

She never saw Mark or that car again.

Angry and intoxicated, Mark stood on the edge of a cliff overlooking the city, preparing to end his life. Suddenly overcome with a sinister rationale, Mark said to himself, "Why am I the one who is dying here? I've done nothing wrong. I'm not the one who deserves to die."

And with that, Mark turned around and left the cliff.

Two weeks later he sat at the man's kitchen table with a soda and a sawed-off shotgun, waiting for him to arrive home.

One wrong deserved another. Eye for eye, and tooth for tooth.

Inside the back cover of that thick Bible was a suicide note Mark had written to his girlfriend. She had been looking for her car for several days until she found the note, and although she didn't understand his intention, she knew he was in danger, so she called the police and reported the car stolen.

When Mark was apprehended and the car found in his possession, she submitted the Bible to the police as evidence of Mark's frame of mind and his plan to commit suicide.

In that first meeting in the gymnasium, I asked Mark to explain why, among all the physical evidence in this case, do the police have a Bible? His response was something I will never forget. His mood changed and with a strange, venomous anger, he leaned out of his chair, pointed a finger in my face. His mouth frothed.

"You ask me about God? I don't know God!" he growled through clenched teeth. His face flushed red and his fists pumped like pistons at his sides. "I wish I knew God! I wouldn't be here if I had known God!"

Then he threw himself back in his chair and stared at me.

Even now, I can feel my breath catch when I remember Mark's outburst, so much like the feeling of staring at the drug dealer's revolver through the tinted window of my car.

From that burst of rage and the details of the murder he had just confessed to, I agreed one-hundred percent with Mark—he didn't know God.

I won't lie and say I felt relaxed after that. In the drama of the moment and the adrenaline dump afterwards, it was not until I got back to my car that I remembered what God had impressed upon me about Mark.

This was the first time that I knew—I mean I really knew—what God intended to use me for in my career as a private detective, newly walking with Him.

I would be the guy who comes alongside offenders and introduces them to God.

Chapter 6
IMPORTANT WORK

"Blessed are the merciful, for they shall receive mercy."
—Matthew 5:7

When Joe's dream to become a state trooper died, he was determined to follow that dream into the grave. During much of his short life, Joe revered the men and women who served in law enforcement as heroes, idols. They were strong, savvy, and true in their work; they helped others in time of need; they kept people safe. Most of all, their work was important. Joe wanted to be involved in important work.

We rarely see the fragility in a man—the cracks and flaws concealed by strong biceps and chiseled good looks. Behind the mystique of a quiet, contemplative demeanor may be an undiagnosed genius or wit, or silent fearful insecurity. For a wanna-be hero like Joe, the ugliest stain on his character would be to show weakness. Like me and so many others, Joe's pretext left people thinking he was a successful young man: healthy, physically strong, an intelligent college graduate with a beautiful fiancée and a wonderful family legacy. He seemed to have all four wheels solidly rolling down the road of life, and all the lights were green.

It's hard to imagine that a change to just one aspect of life could outweigh all of these blessings, but it depends on what that change is. For Joe, that life change was his mom's health. Perhaps Joe was enamored of police officers as helpful heroes as a result of the sincere care for others he saw in his mom when he was growing up. From her, he had developed an almost childlike love for others and a desire to help them. She was the strongest person he had ever known, but when she suffered an aneurism, she became incapable of helping even herself.

Joe's tender heart became clogged with pain, but he never showed it.

Instead, he carried on, completing a degree in criminal justice at one of the premier schools for emerging police professionals, and abusing alcohol as a way to distract himself from worry and sadness.

Without any hesitation Joe admitted he was most angry with God for taking his mother's beautiful mind and heart, but leaving her flesh and failing muscles.

Joe's pattern of drinking eventually led him to develop a tolerance to alcohol. Though building up a tolerance to alcohol doesn't necessarily mask the physiological and neurological effects of the drink, it does make an impact on the level of physical impairment a person feels. In other words, if a person drinks two beers every day for a month, he may need more beer the following month to gain the same feeling of relaxation or happiness that he felt from two beers the previous month. Two beers become three, then four, then more.

Joe had become one of those drinkers who did not feel the physical effects as strongly, even though for his body weight and the amount he consumed, he could be above the legal limit for driving a car.

As a way to neutralize his addiction and unsafe driving habits, Joe ranked himself low against other substance abusers and criminals: Drug dealers? Bad. Dopers? Bad. Murderers? Bad. Joe? Good.

He had no idea that he was literally one turn away from becoming what he judged.

On a very foggy summer morning—the kind of morning when the temperature makes you sweat even before the sun comes up—Joe was driving home from an all-night reunion with a buddy on leave from the service. They had met up nearly twelve hours earlier, when the sun was still shining. They drank a toast and then grabbed some beers and hit the road. They had driven these roads with beer cans between their knees for many years, probably before they were even legally old enough to drink. "Roadies" were part of the rural culture for young men, and a designated driver was the guy who was least drunk at the end of the night.

Their celebration continued when some other friends invited them to a roadhouse. When that bar closed around 1 a.m., the party drifted down to the creek, where they built a fire and went for a dip.

Joe had worked all day. He got home and hit the gym. He was in peak condition as he prepared to take the police cadet exam and physical fitness test. He drank no more and no less than his friends that night, but by the time they got to the roadhouse and were there for a few hours, Joe had slowed down and was ready for bed. When he climbed from the creek, he was relaxed, exhausted, and at his limit for everything. While some of his friends hooked up with local girls, Joe got a ride back to the roadhouse where his sedan was parked, and then he headed for home.

Joe and his fiancée both had the next day off, and their plan was to pick out wedding rings and then go to dinner and a movie. She was beautiful, and he was proud to be faithful to her, even as various drunken girls had presented themselves as opportunity at the roadhouse. He planned to go home, let the dog out, and blast the air conditioner for a few hours of rest before she would arrive around 9 a.m.

Joe descended a long straightaway off the mountain, emerging out of dense fog and into the thick hazy heat. The horizon was only slightly less gray than the sky.

The onboard computer in his car, a vehicular black box similar to a jetliner, would say that Joe was traveling at or slightly greater than the posted speed limit along that road. The computer recorded the last six minutes of Joe's ride home, including radio volume, the position of his driver's side window, and the setting of the car's comfort controls and interior temperature.

Not far from the bottom of the mountain was a slight and sweeping left curve. Joe would navigate this turn and, in a few hundred yards, he'd be at an intersection only two minutes away from his home, dog, and air-conditioned bedroom.

The computer showed that his foot had come off the accelerator even though the car's speed had remained constant, declining only slightly by friction, though the downhill slope was steady. There was no video image, no drive-cam, no traffic cam, no satellite or media recreation of events.

Because his eyes had been closed, Joe only recalled hearing a terrible sound followed by pain in his head and a floating feeling. Then suddenly more noise, his body being sucked into the seat, and the pain of the seatbelt.

At that sweeping left turn, he had fallen asleep.

Joe climbed from his destroyed sedan onto the blacktop and into the hot night. Disoriented, he walked toward the intersection, his last turn home. Realizing this was futile, he turned back up the highway toward a house he knew. A man with a flashlight met him.

In that light, Joe could see the extent of the wreckage. Most of the driver's side had been sheared off like a meat slicer had carved a sliver of steel. A front wheel was missing. The airbag had not deployed and Joe's head had absorbed plastic and broken glass from the car's interior. He had slept through the crash for only a few seconds, maybe four or five, according to the computer's register of normalcy, then no acceleration pedal, then a slight decrease in speed, seconds coasting, then suddenly ground speed ended and the computer systems failed.

"Are you all right?" the man asked, shining the light toward Joe's face.

A voice in the dark distance yelled, "Should I call 911?"

Joe told the man he thought he was all right. The man looked him over and shouted back into the dark that his wife should call 911.

"What did you hit?"

"I must have fallen asleep. I think I hit the bank on the turn up there."

The man shined his light up the roadway along the fog line, illuminating a swath of destroyed brush, torn up sod, and broken vehicle debris.

In the dimmest reach of the flashlight's beam was the reflection of taillights.

The man quickened his pace and Joe staggered beside him. As they got closer, they could clearly see the taillights of a smaller car. As they rushed to the car, the sounds of a man suffering inside became louder and louder.

Joe swayed with fear and disbelief. The lightening sky began to slowly reveal the carnage. Joe could see that the driver's side of the little car had been sliced open, too, but the driver's body had been caught in that carving. He was badly torn and suffering terribly. Anguish spread through Joe's gut and chest. He stood speechless, then talked to the driver frantically, then stared helplessly.

The man with the flashlight ran back to his house to let 911 know there was a second vehicle involved in the crash and that it was very bad. Meanwhile, minutes passed, and Joe tried desperately to help, but he could not patch the driver, nor remove the driver from the twisted metal. He couldn't do anything but stare.

Over the hill, a neighbor had heard the crash and knew immediately it was the sound of two vehicles colliding. He had also called 911 and gave an approximate location, and then he got in his pickup and drove to the scene. By now, first responders had arrived and someone peeled Joe back to a seat on the opposite guardrail, where he sat, shoulders heaving with gut-wrenching sobs.

Emergency responders had arrived quickly. They cut off the driver's side door and loaded the driver into the ambulance. As it was leaving, the ambulance drove over broken glass and debris, and the four tires popped. A second ambulance arrived soon after, and they transferred the driver. The hospital was almost 30 minutes by road and the helicopter couldn't fly because of the fog.

By sunrise Joe wanted to die.

An hour after sunrise, the driver did.

The man with the flashlight and the other neighbor both described Joe as sickened with grief. People at the scene took turns trying to console him, and when police arrived, Joe was put into the backseat of the cruiser and secured for his own protection until investigators could sort out what had happened.

There is a terribly small margin between our futures and that one instance, that one thing that alters our destinies entirely. For truly tenderhearted men, this becomes a breaking point. It is the point where future and life and potential and dreams die, and we want to follow. Strong men put guns to their heads or in their mouths. They jump from heights or walk into traffic. Women take these same extremes, though many times by less graphic means. It's sad to consider how people can feel this is their only solution. The sadness and loss within their broken hearts is incalculable.

When Joe learned he had killed another man, his life essentially ended. He hated himself for what he had done. Though his dreams of policing had been destroyed, it hardly seemed to matter in comparison. In one brief instant, he lost his dreams, all hope, and any self-respect he had remaining in his life.

The police took him for a blood test at the hospital, and Joe was charged with vehicular homicide while driving drunk.

When a man determines to take his life, there are often signs that the family members and friends missed. Sadly, sometimes there are no indications. The person hides his brokenness behind an "I will survive" attitude, and then suddenly ends his life. Other times, the suicide is so slow, death comes after a lifetime of killing oneself.

I believe my grandfather died this way.

When my grandfather, whose nickname was "Dude," and my grandmother married, they went on a two-week honeymoon back to their hometown to visit some family members. They traveled by train. On their return to the train station they were greeted by about fifty friends who had gathered to sing and toast the newlyweds. Grandma's brother-in-law, Wilbur, had driven there to pick them up. Maybe journalism standards weren't what they are today, but the article didn't make it clear who was driving the car when they left the station. The article only referred to the driver as "he," so it could have been Wilbur, or it could have been Dude.

Also different from today's journalism, a young disabled boy in the story was given the harsh label of "cripple." He was specifically mentioned because he was unable to move from in front of the car due to his disability. As the happy couple departed, they accidentally drove over the boy. Frantic, someone picked up the boy and threw him inside the car, and the car raced for the hospital, only a few miles away. I want to believe that Dude picked up the boy and heroically took the wheel. But in this story there are no heroes.

The car reached the end of the road, and as they exited the train depot, the high speed and urgency caused them to lose control. They crashed into a pole.

The boy died.

That was how my grandparents started their life together.

When I was very young, I had found an award that had been given to my great-uncle Wilbur: 50 years without an accident. It was from an insurance company. As a kid, who didn't drive and had no idea what car insurance was, I had no idea the significance of this award.

Now it takes on a whole new meaning.

Though the article didn't specify, I am heartbroken to believe Dude was the driver. Dude, a young, handsome man with a beautiful new wife and bright future, had killed the boy.

Though my uncle's driving award seems to assure this fact, I am more persuaded by the way Dude lived the next thirty years of his life. Though he didn't use a gun or a rope or a razor to take his life, he poisoned himself day after day, year after year, decade after decade, with hard liquor. Before noon, Dude was a tremendous business man. By noon he was a drinker. In the afternoon, he was debilitated drunk. And at night he was an absent parent, and he was the dad my mom deeply loved and wanted to know.

My mom rarely spoke about her dad. Others who knew him told me plenty of stories, rumors, and some great testimony about how truly generous, caring, and humble Dude really was. Dude gave generously to families in need; he even bought land so that it could be modified from a farm into a recreation park with sports fields and ice skating and a playground.

Every drink he took and every bottle he finished numbed him to the guilt and haunting of that boy he killed at the train station the day he came home from his honeymoon. Every generous offering to others was atonement as he struggled to forgive himself. Dude did not go home from the train station in grief and end his life. He did it slowly, and though the history books barely have this legacy, people knew Dude as a wonderful kindhearted man who drank himself to death.

The story of the boy at the train depot was hidden in a newspaper at the historical society in the hometown where my grandparents honeymooned. It was a light of truth that suddenly illuminated why Dude drank so much. Now I know he drank to cope with guilt and trauma. I finally had a glimpse into the heart of a man I never knew. Dude had died when my mother was still in college.

Joe carried this same guilt and trauma. He had not only killed a man, but a hard-working, blue-collar, family man. The man was on his way to work. He got up at four in the morning to have coffee and read his Bible and then drive an hour to be at work by six thirty. He did this six days a week. And the man left behind a wife and sons and granddaughters and friends…a lot of friends.

The man with the flashlight would shake his head and say, "It's a one in a million shot that these two would meet in this exact spot on an open highway in the night, and he would hit him in that exact spot right where his body was and not in front and not in back, but straight on."

Joe described two very long days between the accident and the end. Family members kept him guarded. He did not drink to ease the pain the way he drank to kill the powerlessness and grief he felt over his mother's living death from the aneurysm. He did not talk, did not love, did not feel anything with those around him. His friends offered support, but this was beyond their powers. His boss gave him space, but now work didn't matter. Life was over. He was just looking for a route to take and a time without supervision when he could give up.

On the day I met Joe, he was smiling. He was matter of fact. He was sober, and his eyes led me to believe he was free of anxiety meds and antidepressants. It's rare to meet someone under the burden of taking a life who carries this weight so lightly.

Joe's attorney asked me to sort through the case and come back with my own report. In detective jargon, this is known as a parallel investigation. It doesn't necessarily infer that the first investigation, the police investigation, is flawed or incorrect. The parallel investigation is simply an independent verification of the police investigation that also uncovers additional facts or witnesses who could further complete the full truth. Interviewing Joe was my first step.

One benefit of being a PI is having access to the full truth. I've joked that the only people more knowledgeable than me of any case are the victim, the offender, and God. Unfortunately, in many cases, the victim is dead, and the offender may be truthful except for those things concealed in his heart. This brings me back to God. I pray to God for help. I ask God to keep me safe, my heart and my mind, as well as my physical body. And I pray for God to help me to understand what I am supposed to do in every case that I work. God is faithful, and He always helps me.

Joe's attorney mentioned that Joe was remorseful and that he was messed up over the crash. I asked if he had any lingering injuries and the attorney snapped back, "No, he's just messed up—he killed a man!"

The man standing in front of me didn't seem messed up, though.

"You seem to be doing pretty well," I said to Joe.

"I am. I know what I did and I'm willing to take accountability, so whatever your investigation is, I will help you get to the truth, but I'm planning to plead guilty anyway."

I explained to him some legal points and some facts about how learning more about the crash and verifying police information would help his attorney with representation. If there was any mercy the court could have on his charges or his sentence, the independent investigation would help with that.

I drew his attention to the police report. The officer had written that witnesses and people on scene were concerned that he was going to try to harm himself. I questioned his state of mind. Joe discussed his desire for suicide with scary candor. Then he concluded that those feelings had passed.

"I had fully planned to kill myself, and my fiancée took me to see her pastor, and I accepted Jesus Christ as my Lord and Savior. I know that God is going to help me through this."

I closed my office door so people wouldn't be scared from the sight of two grown men crying.

He continued, "I learned that the man I killed was a man who walked with God and I know that he was a forgiving man. People have told me a lot about him in these months, and I know I need peace the way he had peace, even after what I did to him."

Hearing all of this overwhelmed me and I admit that talking about God was far from my mind when Joe walked into my office. We spent the next hour talking about Joe's salvation and his baptism. He told me how his conversion had strengthened his relationship with his fiancée, and how growing into a strong Christian man was diluting his pain and fear of prison. Like water mixing with alcohol, even the pain Joe had for both his mother's condition and the loss of his dream as a police officer were diluted by God.

In our second hour together, Joe was able to concisely discuss the twenty-four hours prior to the accident. This is a critical time period for the investigation because understanding the prior day's activities help to explain physical condition and emotions. Was there malice? Was there injury or exhaustion? Were there emotions or other factors that could be relevant in understanding criminal intent? When alcohol is a central factor, it's important to understand the prior day's diet because it has an impact on the metabolism of alcohol.

During such explanations, I look for contradictions and lies. Offenders, even Christian offenders, are human and often try to paint themselves in the most favorable light possible, even when confessing.

Joe maintained that he had fallen asleep. He intended to plead guilty because it was the right thing to do for taking a man's life.

I walked with Joe out of the office and down to his work truck. He said he was still uneasy driving and hyper-vigilant now, and I could understand how he would feel that way. I put my hand on his shoulder and we prayed. I concluded with a rephrase of a familiar Scripture: "If God is with us, who cares who's against us" (Romans 8:31)? I could feel God's presence, and I was eager to help his case. I abandoned my schedule, grabbed my camera bag, and within a few hours, I was at the scene and talking to the man who had held the flashlight and instructed his wife to call 911 when he saw the crash.

During this timeframe, the wife of the man Joe killed had heard about Joe giving his life to the Lord. Because it was a small community, she learned about the climb Joe had made from the depths of suicide. People from her family and church had looked into the sincerity of his reformation. She knew Joe struggled with finding peace and that his confession and guilty plea were establishing a foundation for forgiveness.

That word forgiveness was such an amazing but foreign concept to Joe. He needed to know that the wife forgave him; he yearned for confirmation that his victim would have forgiven him; he prayed that their family and friends would forgive him. And he prayed their forgiveness would not be fake or meaningless. Though he had experienced the darkness of depression, Joe had never before wanted to hurt himself. He had always dreamed of that police career and of doing important work that would help others. Instead, he would now be facing life from the other side of the prison bars, and he anticipated suffering in the hell of state prison for many years.

He had no idea what his victim's wife would do. Like so many victims, she had every right, both legally and morally, to stand in court, cry, scream, and shake her fist at Joe as she described for the judge in sorrowful detail the emotional, relational, and financial loss she had suffered because Joe had been drinking and fallen asleep. He anticipated listening to her explain how brokenhearted she was because her best friend, the father of her children, and her soulmate, had been snatched away from her by a drunk driver. She had every right to hate him, to want him to rot in prison for the maximum sentence.

But instead, she went to the prosecutor and asked for mercy. She told him that she and her husband were both Christians, and that Joe had recently become a Christian, too. Her faith compelled her toward forgiveness, and she wanted Joe to feel the tangible effects of God's forgiveness through others. She wanted to strengthen the young man's new faith and express her own. She believed this is what her husband would have wanted her to do.

The prosecutor took her request to the judge.

The circumstances surrounding Joe's crime provided for a prison sentence as short as seven years and as long as fifteen. Because of the wife's plea, Joe's sentence was reduced to three years.

In court, those who speak are said to give testimony. Christians also give testimony. In both cases, testimony is the truth and it is given under an oath. In court you pledge that you will not lie to the judge. The judge hears what you say, as do jurors and other attorneys. The prosecutor will ask you questions about your testimony to punch holes in your logic and get you to contradict yourself, all in an attempt to discredit you. But when your testimony is the truth, it can't be discredited.

When you give testimony about God and about the conversion of your life from sinner to salvation, there is often the same type of analysis. However, instead of God being involved as a witness of intimidation who will send lightning bolts or earthquakes on you for perjury in court, God is like a rejoicing symphony conductor or a gigantic voice on a stadium loudspeaker shouting cheers of excitement. I like those guys in the Bible who are challenged by non-believers and cynics, and their testimony is not qualified by "swearing" or "put your right hand on this stack of Bibles, sir." Peter and John said without intimidation, "…we cannot help speaking about what we have seen and heard" (Acts 4:20, NIV).

In court, the wife *was* overcome with emotion. So much so that she gave a letter to the best friend of the man Joe killed because she was too choked up to speak. The letter was simple in words and detailed in facts. It was truthful and amazing; in it, she described her love for her husband, their love for God, and her faith that he didn't suffer in death because of God.

Joe stood with his attorney and he looked at the family and at the friend who recited the wife's statement. I stood by his side, washed in God's Spirit. God was palpably in the courtroom. Instead of the burden of condemnation, the weighty presence of God's glory filled the place. The word 'forgiveness' resounded over and over as the friend read the letter.

Because the session was a DWI offender court, the courtroom was full of people who had been charged for driving while intoxicated. Men and women, young and old, some first-time offenders, some second-time or even third—they all sat quietly and heard the message of the letter.

Though dozens of people were present that day, Joe was the only defendant who had killed someone.

As the letter was read, the judge's face became red with emotion. It was obvious he was fighting back tears as he listened to the message of grace from the victim's family.

After the letter, Joe spoke. He confessed in a few concise sentences that he drank too much…that what he had done brought pain to two families. He spoke about the driver, the man he killed. He called him by his first name and expressed that he wanted to know the same truth and salvation that his victim had. Then Joe gave his testimony of turning his life to God.

Joe apologized with sober intensity and told the judge that he was prepared to be accountable for his crime.

After more than twenty years in this job, I had never seen anything like it in court.

An unusual silence followed his statement, and, not knowing what to do, Joe continued speaking about how much he appreciates forgiveness and what God has done for his life.

Also unusual, the judge did not let Joe sit down or order him to be shackled and removed.

He let Joe stand and asked the audience, "How many of you are here on your first DWI? If you are, stand up."

He waited until all of the first-time offenders stood. Then he asked the second-time offenders to stand. Then the third.

By the time the judge was done, almost the entire courtroom was standing with Joe.

The judge then turned to Joe and asked, "Have you ever been arrested?"

"No, Your Honor."

"You weren't expecting this to happen, were you?

"No, Your Honor."

"This has changed your life forever, hasn't it?"

"Yes, Your Honor."

Then the judge turned his gaze again to the audience.

"Ladies and gentlemen in the courtroom, take a good hard look at this man who stands before you and think about your own life. This is what could happen the next time you decide to drive after drinking. And this is only his first offense."

A heavy, sober silence hung in the courtroom before the judge thanked Joe for his testimony and remanded him to the custody of the sheriff's office.

Joe thanked his attorney, shook my hand, and hugged his father, sister, and fiancée. The deputy politely took him by the arm and walked him to a back room and out of sight. Both families followed behind Joe. The victim's wife and family wiped at tears.

Though forgiveness had ruled the day, it was not without pain. In the hallway, Joe's fiancée screamed his name in anguish, the reality of not seeing him as a free man for three years suddenly crashing down on her. His family hugged her, stroked her hair, and muffled her cries in their shoulders. As they walked away, her lonely wails faded down the hallway and outside of the courthouse.

A few hours later, I was at the correctional facility where Joe had been taken. I was interviewing another inmate when the deputies brought Joe into the intake area on the other side of the glass. He looked at me with surprise and smiled. On the way out, I walked past him, and a guard asked if I knew him.

I said, "Oh yeah, we just came from court. You won't have any trouble with this guy. He's all right." Joe was smiling when I last saw him and he gave me a thumb pointing up to the God who had saved him.

CHAPTER 7

BETWEEN THE DOORS

"But you are a chosen race, a royal priesthood, a holy nation, a people for his own possession, that you may proclaim the excellencies of him who called you out of darkness into his marvelous light. Once you were not a people, but now you are God's people; once you had not received mercy, but now you have received mercy."
—1 Peter 2:9-10

Eighteen months passed between the time Mark was captured and when the judge imposed a life sentence for first degree murder. For Mark, that time plodded by. He cycled through several county jails while he awaited trial. This was not an unusual time period, though, because death penalty cases include many procedural stages to assure a fair trial. The sixth amendment of the Constitution frames these due process rights and protections, and precedent set by previous court rulings and recommendations from the American Bar Association further guide the process.

When I was appointed to Mark's case, my original job was to gather facts, review evidence, and conduct a parallel investigation. The goal of this work was to provide an expert perspective for the defense attorneys to consider. My late friend Rick, an investigator I had admired my whole career but had only recently become friends with in the years before his death, referred to the importance of "fresh eyes" on a case. This was exactly why I was appointed to Mark's case: to offer a fresh perspective that could help the attorneys analyze the evidence from a different perspective.

My investigation was straightforward because Mark didn't hesitate to admit his crime, and the evidence supported his admission of guilt. But Mark also didn't hesitate to admit his motive for the crime; in fact, he seemed proud that he had achieved his goal—protecting his kids. Over the ten years when Mark was separated from his kids, his family and friends gave him updates about his ex-wife and kids, and his anger grew in tandem with his love for them. Mark saw this murder as an honor killing, for himself and for his children.

Because of this mindset, Mark was eager to take this case to trial. In court he hoped to do two things: tell his story to a sympathetic audience and die for his children. I could relate to both causes, and I became bonded to Mark's case. Though I have never condoned the way Mark handled his problems, I could understand how a desperate man without God could choose such an action. Though Mark and I lived in very different lives, I could still see so much in him that was like me. He had a tough childhood. His father had failed him. He grew up wanting to be loved and respected, and as a young husband and father, the anger and shame in his heart limited that potential.

Despite the fact that Mark might be executed if he were convicted of first degree murder, he still desired to have a relationship with his kids. He rationalized that his death was a noble sacrifice to prove that he loved them above all else, even his own life. He would not die with the legacy of abandonment and indifference that was his father's. In fact, when Mark's father died, Mark was in prison and they had not reconciled. Mark would not die like his father. He would die so his children would know he loved them.

In several meetings, Mark's legal team vividly described death row. The official day of execution would come very slowly, if at all. Time waiting for that ultimate sacrifice would be spent in isolation, absent of human contact. Guards would bring a portable shower to his cell door twice a week for four minutes at a time. Meals would be shoved through a slot on the floor. Attorney phone calls would be the only outside voice he would hear except for occasional chatter among other condemned men and the guards. Mark would never touch another human being again, and if he were to see a family member, it would be only through thick glass or in the audience at a legal proceeding. He would have a right to waive appeals and to ask for a speedy end to his case, but other appeals and constitutional cases could be filed on his behalf by strangers, who hoped to use Mark as their political poster boy for abolition of the death penalty. These cases would tie up Mark's execution in the courts for years, further adding to his misery and barring his goal of self-sacrifice. And if he were depressed by all of this, he could forget suicide as a way out. His cell would be searched regularly, and any means of self-harm would be removed.

And Mark was depressed, well before he received his sentence. In his second jail, the one where our only "private" meeting space was center court in the gym, Mark asked for psychological counseling for his depression and anxiety. In an attempt to save costs associated with a counselor or overtime for staff, the warden reported that Mark was a dangerous inmate due to his psychological issues. Instead of getting him a counselor, the warden transferred him to another jail several hours away. There Mark lived in a more spacious single cell, and he had the opportunity to talk with a young counselor several times a week. Mark admitted that the counseling didn't help, though. He wouldn't open up because he was paranoid that his conversations were monitored or the counselor was actually a police officer in disguise.

It was at this jail that Mark and I got deeper into the mitigating circumstances of his life story. The court had approved a modification in my appointment, and after I testified before a judge about my education and experience, the judge added me as a mitigation expert to help the attorneys' argument against the death penalty. Mark experienced a lot of stress during these conversations. Because I needed to probe sensitive issues regarding his family history, particularly his feelings about his father's abandonment of him, our meetings often ended in fits of rage and Mark's fists pounding on the table.

When I asked Mark, "So you don't think what happened to you as a kid has anything to do with the man you are?" he slammed his fists on the table.

"Listen!" he yelled. "This ain't no fairytale. This here's my life."

I repeated my question, and when he told me again that he saw no connection between his childhood experiences and his choices in adulthood, I shook my head and walked out.

Walking out is not always the best tactic, but it gave me space and allowed Mark to cool down from being emotionally and physically flooded. When communication breaks down in such meetings, ending the conversation and starting fresh when the offender has a chance to process his feelings is an effective strategy. In the meantime, I could continue to investigate Mark's family history, childhood, and adolescent experiences.

Interestingly, many years later, I had a similar experience with another young defendant who faced the death penalty. He answered my questions with shouting and fist-pounding and then refused to speak. I walked out on that guy, too, thinking it would allow him to calm down and consider reality.

I told Mark about that conversation when I visited him at the prison where he had been sentenced, and he explained something very profound that I had never considered. He said the weight of guilt a man feels for killing another man is more real than he lets others see. And the weight of the death penalty on top of that guilt becomes exponentially heavier. Mark said that unless I personally experienced that weight, there is no way I could comprehend the stress and anxiety a man feels in that situation. Yes, I could feel stress for my investigation, and, yes, I could feel stress because there might not be much I could do, but I could still walk out of that jail and go home a free man, in both body and conscience.

When I visited that other client a few weeks later, I apologized for walking out on him. He accepted my apology and then answered my questions.

As Mark's case inched closer to trial, he was moved to a fourth facility. It was modern and offered extensive visitation rooms for the legal team. He still insisted on going to trial. Even with the risk of receiving the death penalty and being in isolation for years, he believed in the importance of telling his story to the public. Mark clung to the belief that when the jury heard what this man had done to his family, they might see the murder as a justifiable means of revenge and give Mark a lesser penalty. The difference would be in how the story was told.

I found myself more engaged in writing Mark's story for his legal team and for the forensic psychiatrist, who would also evaluate his competency and mental health. The dominant theme in Mark's life was abandonment and the absence of family love. All Mark ever wanted was to have a stable loving family. The tragedy in his story is that he achieved this dream and then lost it.

Mark was the youngest of five kids. His father worked in management and his mother was a homemaker. In a classic chain of events, his father had an affair with a secretary and his parents divorced when Mark was a toddler. After the divorce, his mother became a barmaid and, because of her late hours, the kids raised themselves.

When Mark was five years old, he had gone to the city zoo with his older brothers. The brothers dared him to feed a hotdog to a bear inside a cage, so Mark worked his way over some fences and approached the cage bars. He stuck the hotdog through the bars, and the bear quickly bit, tearing off part of Mark's hand in the process.

While he was in the hospital, Mark's father visited for an hour or so. He gave Mark a few toy cars to play with and then went back to his new family in the suburbs. His dad had married the secretary and they had a child together. The injuries to Mark's hand healed.

As a child and teenager, Mark struggled socially. He and his middle brother, Eddie, were close in age and spent a lot of time skipping school, fishing, and exploring on their bicycles. They weren't exactly juvenile delinquents, but they weren't obedient either. Fighting and drinking were easier than going to school. Mark spent a lot of time looking for his dad or trying to forget that his father didn't want him.

Mark's mom drank whenever she was not working. Her shame rested in the loss of her husband and the destruction of her own family when he left his five kids.

I met with a guy who claimed to be one of Mark's truest friends during high school. This guy's family had moved to a small community about thirty miles away from the city, and though they were not rich, they offered Mark their extra bedroom to get him off the street so he could finish high school. Mark accepted the offer and did well in school. He attended church with the family on Sundays.

When he was 16 years old, Mark asked his friend for a ride to visit his father. His friend's dad drove Mark to a house outside of the city, where they found Mark's father splitting firewood in the yard. Mark approached his father and the two stood awkwardly in the yard for a short time. His father never smiled at Mark or hugged him. He offered his son no affection, not even a pat on the shoulder as Mark turned to walk back to the car.

Mark didn't talk the entire ride home. The following day, he thanked his friend and his family for inviting him to stay with them and announced he was going back to the city. When Mark left, his friend remembered him as being emotionally walled off. They knew Mark was heartbroken, but he wouldn't share his feelings with them.

This experience with his dad heaped further rejection upon his early abandonment, and Mark was unable to overcome the shame and pain. Though he was bitter at his father, he didn't hate him and continued to long for a relationship with him. Even when Mark met the love of his life and started a family of his own, he still acutely felt the vacancy of a father, who could have mentored him in being a good husband and parent. Though he struggled with this pain, it didn't diminish Mark's love and enthusiasm for being a father. Mark worked hard and strived to provide a life for his kids, unlike the life he had. School activities, birthday parties, and family gatherings were important events Mark tried never to miss. To others, Mark appeared to have a great family, and in many ways he did, but inside, he was still sad and scarred. He had never shared with anyone, not even his wife or siblings, how deeply his father's rejection had hurt him, how deeply his shame from abandonment dragged at his mental energy and intruded into his thoughts. Instead, he medicated this pain with marijuana and alcohol. This, Mark would later reluctantly observe, caused strain in his marriage.

After many interviews with Mark, his family members, and friends, I was finally able to piece together the story of his life. During one of our meetings, I shared my observations with him, and for the first time, he could see how his pain-filled childhood influenced his adult relationships. In particular, he could understand how his unconfessed shame and unrepented anger had damaged his relationship with his wife, the mother of his children.

At twenty, Mark was attracted to his wife because they had so much in common. She was a few years younger and was grieving the death of her mother. He deeply identified with her unhappiness, dissatisfaction with life, and eagerness for independence, and Mark believed they were ideal life partners. But because he had concealed his true emotions about his father and began abusing substances, confusion, disagreements, and stress began to erode her love for him. Eventually that love was replaced by a desire for more in life. There was an emptiness in her Mark no longer filled, and this need for affection made her vulnerable to the attention of other men.

In court, Mark's story could be told in a number of ways—and the way Mark understood the interconnections among the major events in his life would determine how he would tell his story to the jury. The first choice would be for Mark to testify at his trial and explain his actions and motives. The jury would hear, from his perspective, why he waited ten years and then carefully—through surveillance, intelligence gathering, and the tedious preparations related to the stolen sawed-off shotgun—ambushed and executed a man with multiple, well placed gunshots. Even in Mark's version, the jury would not miss the fact that he fired ten shots. Though Mark hadn't planned for this coincidence, the prosecutor would surely emphasize that point. After Mark told his story to the jury, that same prosecutor would give the jury a definition of first degree murder, and they would convict him of that charge. The jury would not see this act as the merciful honor killing Mark believed it was.

The other option would be for Mark to sit silently and allow the prosecutor to present the very same evidence. Inevitably, the jury would come to the same conclusion, and Mark would be convicted. In the process, the jury would hear a parade of others tell his story, with Mark's ex-wife at the front, ready to tell the jury what a heartless psychopath Mark was for ruining her life. Again, that story would be far different from Mark's story and never capture his goal of protecting his children. Based on this version, the jury would most likely vote for the death penalty.

Mark's best option was to concede his guilt in a plea and accept a life sentence. The option of a life sentence plea deal included benefits Mark had never considered. First, Mark would have the last word in the courtroom, prior to the judge's comments and pronouncement of sentence. Second, Mark would have the opportunity to tell his story in full, without time limit or cross examination. Third, and possibly most importantly, Mark would have the opportunity to deliver a message directly to his children. If he had gone to trial and was convicted, all of the evidence against him would have been laid bare during the proceedings. Such details would surely have horrified his children, and there would have been less of a chance for Mark to communicate his sincere love for his children, which they very much needed to know.

Based on these scenarios, I posed an unbelievable possibility to Mark: as a life inmate, he would still have the opportunity for a relationship with his children. Through the grace of God, it would be possible that his children would forgive him and reconcile with him. He would have the chance to be a father again, even if it meant being behind bars to do so. Such forgiveness and reconciliation might take years, but it was a possibility, and it would be worth the risk.

Mark considered this. On one hand, ending this case would remove the millstone from his neck, and the chance to tell his story and send a message to his kids appealed to him. On the other hand, the temptation to believe that one jury member might pause long enough to say, "If someone did that to me and my family, I'd kill him too," was strong. Only one dissenting juror would keep the jury undecided and avert the death penalty.

The weights bearing down on Mark were oppressive. His love and longing for his children, his guilt for killing the man, and his fear of receiving the death penalty were breaking him mentally and emotionally. Though Mark tried to shoulder these burdens, he was showing signs that they were heavier than he let on. He considered how an admission of guilt would prevent a death penalty ruling, allow him to confront his remorse for the murder, and seek forgiveness from God and others. Because Mark had been enslaved to shame and fear for so long, pleading guilty seemed like the first time he would be in control of his life. In this instance, he would rule his emotions instead of his emotions ruling him.

For several difficult weeks, Mark swung sporadically between pleading guilty and going to trial. I offered to help him write a statement that would include personalized messages to his children. This would be a statement forever preserved in the transcript record of the sentencing hearing. Mark's statement would be filed in the county courthouse, and the media would report highlights. Whether or not his children were present in the courtroom to hear his voice, Mark's words would be as permanent as his love.

The tipping point came during my review of the evidence with him. One of the most challenging aspects of my job involves reviewing crime scene photos. In the college courses that I teach, I am staggered at the number of students who find the gore of homicide and crime scenes to be so intriguing, and I often wonder if the ever-popular crime shows have desensitized them to real-life violence. They have yet to discover how long-lasting those images can be in our memories, or how such images can pop into our thoughts or dreams without warning. I've seen enough to last a lifetime, and I'll never forget the photos I saw of Mark's crime.

When I showed Mark the first photo of his victim, he shut down. Our meeting had begun with Mark angrily insisting to exert his right to trial, but those demands ended seconds later when Mark pushed the photo away and slammed his face onto the desk. He had never sobbed so remorsefully over his crime. Occasionally, he had shed a tear or his voice had shaken, but that day he was crying from a grief and guilt I had never seen in him before.

His only intelligible words were, "I will plead. I want to get this over with."

As he cried, I went to his side, put my hand on his shoulder, and began to pray aloud. I cannot clearly recall my prayer. I only remember asking Jesus to come into his heart, to bring him peace, and to help Mark to believe. Mark reached up and held my hand. I remember his grip and his sincerity. I prayed for God to enter his life and Mark, sobbing, said yes. Though I can't clearly remember the words of my prayer, I can recall that at the very moment Mark recognized the enormity of his crime and acknowledged his sin against this man, and he repented and opened his heart wide to God's love and forgiveness. He could no longer justify his actions, to himself or to anyone else. He needed God to justify him now; he needed God to renew his heart.

When I tell this story, I have to be careful not to boast about "winning a soul" for God. I understand the Great Commission is to go out and make disciples (Mark 16:15), but this does not mean we score points in the number of people we "win" to God. I've heard people say things like, "I saved a soul today," or "I led him to the Lord." Though people mean well with these phrases, this language bothers me. First, we did not hang on a cross and die for the person we prayed for, so we didn't save them. Second, unless the Father draws people to Jesus, they're not able to come to Him (John 6:44), so we didn't technically lead them to Jesus, either. God did. Ultimately, God draws and saves people, and we participate in this process by telling others about Jesus and praying for them. When we speak of others' salvation, we need to be humble, so we don't accidentally believe the glory that actually belongs to God belongs to us.

When Mark repented and believed, it became apparent that over the many months he had spent in prison awaiting trial, God had been drawing him. Over time, God had simply used me to deliver a message of grace and truth to him, and when it was time for Mark to confront the reality of his crime, God's work had come to fruition. I never expected God to save him during that meeting, and I couldn't have planned it. Mark's salvation was a miracle, and I found incredible joy in what God had done.

For the first time in his life, Mark had a Father who loved him.

The conference room was private, except for the glass walls that enclosed it behind a heavy, locking steel door. This room was part of a pod of windowed conference rooms, and guards sat in a control room overlooking this area. Other than the table and our two chairs, the only other fixtures in the room were a phone and a big red panic button on the far wall. And though this room had no video cameras or microphones in it, the guards still had a clear view of us.

My arm was wrapped around Mark's shoulders, and his head was down on the table. His hand held mine. When Mark confidently asked for God to come into his heart and to help him, I stood up, excited about what had just happened. As we talked, I told Mark I would pass along his decision to plead guilty to the attorneys, and I promised to help him write his confession statement to the court.

Though this may seem like a benign situation, I violated prison rules because I had direct physical contact with an inmate. Beyond a professional handshake, members of the legal team are not allowed to touch inmates, and they are not to be any closer than what is necessary in order to share legal documents. Our body postures and movements had caught the guards' attention. Mark's head and body were out of their view from the control room; I was standing over him with my head close to his; and I had moved away from him abruptly. They probably believed we were fighting and I was in danger.

After we finished praying, Mark looked completely different. There was an expression on his face that radiated peace. He didn't look like the angry prisoner I had been meeting with for months. It was a look of freedom.

I was so overjoyed by the change in his face that I shouted, "This is what I mean about peace in your heart!"

Mark smiled because I had said that to him many times: "I pray for peace in your heart."

When I shouted "peace in your heart," the metal door to the conference room clicked open and echoed loudly. It was a well-timed entrance, because I humorously equate the unlocking of that door with Mark's soul becoming free. The two large corrections officers who ran into the pod weren't in nearly as humorous a frame of mind, however. I scooped up all of the documents and photos from the table and packed them into my file case as the first officer opened the door.

"Is everything all right in here?" the first officer asked me.

"Yeah, everything is fine. We were just wrapping up. He's ready to go back to his cell."

I said goodbye to Mark and walked a few steps to the portal exiting from the pod, and the door was already buzzing, waiting for me to push through. I secured the door, slamming it closed, and waited a few seconds in the cube for the second door to open and let me into the lobby.

Being between the doors was a normal part of my job. As I stepped into the lobby, though, I realized that Mark had been trapped between his own doors for some time—trapped between wanting to justify his crime and humbly admitting his guilt. Mark was finally willing to walk through the second door and admit his guilt that day, and it radically changed the outcome of his case, both here and in eternity. Though Mark was going back inside the prison to his cell, in his spirit, he was a free man.

CHAPTER 8
MERCY

"Let us then with confidence draw near to the throne of grace, that we may receive mercy and find grace to help in time of need."
—Hebrews 4:16

om's life was decaying all around him. Though he worked hard as a physical laborer, his workdays were drenched in coffee to soak up the booze from each night's binges. He drank to overcome the stress of his job and to stave off painful memories from the past. He knew he needed to be rescued from this cycle of pain and substance abuse—he couldn't end it on his own. And he knew God could help him. Though he wasn't raised in church and didn't even own a Bible, he just knew that God could rescue people.

But Tom wouldn't ask God for help.

He didn't think he knew God's language.

When Tom had heard people pray in the past, they had sounded eloquent, educated, and coherent. TV and radio preachers spoke powerful, reverent-sounding prayers; families holding hands around a Norman Rockwell-style dinner table bowed their heads in humble, heartfelt prayers. In comparison to these picture-perfect prayers, Tom felt dumb. He was intimidated and feared he could never string together a respectful, holy sentence that would be worthy of God's attention.

So instead, Tom remained silent to God and let his life continue to descend deeper and deeper into misery.

Tom believed there was only one way to pray to God, and it required much preparation and formality if he had any hopes of his prayers being received. He didn't live in holiness. His clothing was worn and his hands usually dirty. His voice was rough and his breath often smelled like tobacco and alcohol. He couldn't go more than a few sentences without cursing. And he feared that once he opened his heart, the tears he had kept deep in his heart all of his life would never stop. He didn't trust that God would hear him if he wailed incoherently and hyperventilated single syllable words.

Tom's story could have turned out so differently if he had given prayer a try. Likewise, it would have helped Tom if someone who knew the truth about prayer had encouraged him to pray. Tom desperately needed to hear that God loves our voices no matter how roughly we communicate and no matter how inexperienced we are at praying.

Like Tom, so many people allow their lives to be destroyed because they don't pray, thinking they don't know what to say to God. Not only are they afraid God won't listen, they fear the ridicule of others who might hear them call out to God for help. They don't want to be laughed at when their words become mixed up in a salad of incomprehension. Because so many people believe calling for help is a sign of weakness, they also believe calling out to God in a disorganized prayer compounds the humiliation.

They don't know how to begin or who to address.

"God, it's me…"

"Jesus, please help me…"

"Holy Spirit, come to me. I'm in big trouble here…"

Men die because they are afraid of being wrong in what they say in prayer to God. No one ever taught them to pray. Some even believe the only one who can pray is a religious leader, and so they become reliant on others to pray for them. They're unwilling to even try, because the words don't flow as smoothly as the priest or the pastor.

And on top of his insecurities about the words to say, Tom believed he didn't deserve God's help. He had lived his entire life void of morality, structure, and respect for others. To believe that now, in desperate circumstances, praying was going to matter seemed hypocritical and pointless. Thus, he further justified his silence toward God with a backwards form of humility: I deserve to suffer; God won't listen to someone like me; why would he want to answer my prayer? He probably hates me for what I've done.

And Tom had done something that caused a lot of pain.

He had killed a woman who was riding a motorcycle with her grandchild.

Drunk on rum, Tom had careened through an intersection and slammed directly into Gloria and her grandson. Gloria died on impact, her head and neck pounding into the hood of his car before she rolled to the street.

When Tom collided with Gloria, cars jammed their brakes and peeled to the roadsides. An off-duty police officer ran from his pickup truck toward the scene to offer assistance. Gloria's body lay in the intersection, her motorcycle splayed in pieces across the asphalt.

Tom felt the rum and tried to clear his head, but he couldn't get sober. He knew Gloria was dead, and he walked in wobbly, anxious circles around her until he saw the boy.

Miraculously, her grandson landed on the lush grass nearby, completely unharmed.

Tom stumbled toward the boy, who knelt on the grass, stunned and screaming.

The officer, who believed that Tom was running away, grabbed him and placed him on the ground. But the officer was wrong.

Tom didn't want to run. He wanted to die.

In my first meeting with Tom, he said, "I took enough drugs and alcohol to kill myself time and time again, and I never died. The only person I ever wanted to hurt was me." He paused for a long moment. His voice wavered and a tear escaped. "I wish I knew the reason God never took me. There must be some purpose to my life. I wish I knew what it was."

That first tear had seeped through the wall around Tom's heart. He had always feared that wall would crumble, and when it did, a flood of weeping was unleashed.

I sat close to Tom and prayed with him. Tom was no longer self-conscious about how formal his language was. Through gasps and tears, he asked Jesus to tell him why he had been spared but Gloria had died.

When Tom killed Gloria, he had no idea she was a Christian. Gloria loved God, pure and simple. She taught her sons that trusting God, having faith, and practicing forgiveness were the keys to a good life, both here and after death. When Gloria died, she was ready and eager to meet God, by all accounts, especially her own.

By the end of our meeting, Tom had a new faith in God. He had grieved his actions and believed that God would forgive him and rescue him from sin. But Tom was not attempting to be rescued from the consequences of what he had done. He agreed to take full responsibility for the accident, plead guilty, and prepare himself for prison time. Tom acknowledged that to really understand his purpose in life, he would need to be accountable to something besides himself and the bottle. For the first time, he felt forgiven by God.

God had heard his prayers.

But the days ahead were not entirely free from depression and fear as Tom began to feel the weight of having killed another human being. Tom was deeply thankful and humbled that God had forgiven him, but he struggled with how he felt about himself. For the first few days following Gloria's death, he lay on the sofa inside his trailer. He didn't eat. He kept the door open, and neighbors came regularly to tap on the screen door to check on him. Tom would moan and tell them to go away. His friends, the people he had been drinking rum and beer with a few days earlier, had quit calling. Tom had drunk enough rum and beer with them to have over twice the legal limit of alcohol in his blood when he killed Gloria. He was glad to be rid of his "friends" and their influence.

Tom kept a gun near his side, but a neighbor took it away for fear he would use it.

On that sofa, Tom did little else except ruminate about the accident, his painful past, and the terror that would be his future behind bars.

Like so many other offenders, Tom's past was filled with horrific, ongoing abuse.

Tom's father had been a Marine during the Vietnam War. Part of his duty included standing watch on the ship during the night while the ship was anchored in port. Watch duty involved both armed patrol of the ship's deck and surrounding water, and also being alert for saboteurs, who frequently attempted to plant explosives on the ship.

Sailors and Marines were authorized to shoot saboteurs without warning.

On a moonless night, Tom's father caught a glimpse of a shadowy figure climbing onto the deck near the ship's bow. As trained, he shouted to alert others to the intruder and then opened fire with his rifle. When the echo of the gunfire ceased, all that was heard was the splash of a body hitting the water. The crew stood alert until daylight, when divers went into the water and recovered the body of the saboteur.

On the deck, the security detail examined the small body dressed in all black. A scarf covered the man's head, and a small backpack was still strapped to his back. The bullet wound was a clean shot through his torso. Everyone thought Tom's father had stopped a bomb from being planted on the boat. He had saved the ship and crew.

Then they pulled off the scarf and examined the face. The saboteur was a young village woman. When they opened her backpack, it contained a few pieces of waterlogged fruit and some packaged food with U.S. Navy markings.

Also inside the backpack, wrapped in some rags, was a baby.

The woman was not a saboteur but a hungry mother with her baby, raiding ships at night to find food. When Tom's father shot her, she fell into the water and the baby drowned.

The Marines had to remove Tom's father from duty, and he spent a year in a psychiatric hospital in California before he returned home. His father drank heavily to numb his guilt, and when he was drunk, he would beat Tom and his mother in rage. During one of those fits of rage, Tom's father kicked his wife in the stomach and then threw her down the cellar steps. She was several months pregnant with Tom's younger sister, and when she gave birth, his sister was severely disabled.

Not too long after this, Tom's parents divorced.

Tom's teenage years were divided between caring for his sister and struggling to become the man his mother's new boyfriend expected him to be. Tom was emotionally sensitive, much like his mother. He was already traumatized from physical abuse as well as from the many nights his father made him sit at the kitchen table while his dad drank liquor and repeated the story of killing the saboteur over and over.

But with his mom's new boyfriend, Sawyer, the kitchen table had become the place where Sawyer and his brothers would drink liquor, play cards, and laugh raucously late into the night. Though Tom was underage, they served him whiskey and encouraged him to drink until he became a comedic sideshow for Sawyer and his friends. They would laugh and enjoy the spectacle of Tom making a fool of himself. Tom would eventually pass out on the floor and sleep until school the next day.

When he got older, Tom spent his summers working on a crew at a lumberyard where Sawyer was foreman. Tom stacked boards from age 11 until he was about 15 years old. The men would drink beer during lunch, and Tom was allotted one beer per day; however, he was soon keeping pace with Sawyer and his friends who regularly downed six-packs at lunch.

His mom and Sawyer eventually got married, and when Tom was in high school, they moved to rural Tennessee. Although he had been working in the lumberyard for many years, Tom was still a chubby boy with the emotional tendencies of his mother. In Tennessee, the schools were undergoing integration, and race relations were on shaky ground. One day, a group of black students attacked Tom on the school bus, and when the principal investigated, Tom was blamed for making racial slurs. The principal spoke with him and soon realized the intolerant attitude came from Tom's step-father, Sawyer. The principal excused the incident and helped Tom with an apology to the black students.

Unfortunately, this issue rose again and again, becoming a torment to Tom. Sawyer was furious when Tom wouldn't fight back, going so far as to show up at the bus stop one day to make sure Tom fought back. When Tom refused, Sawyer himself struck Tom, and he fell to the ground as the bus pulled away.

In a particularly harsh incident, one of the black students hit Tom with a plastic slat from a field fence, leaving a painful, scarring welt on his leg. Angry that Tom had been assaulted by a black student, Sawyer arranged for a meeting with the principal. In the meeting Sawyer became enraged. The principal told Sawyer that fighting would not be tolerated at school, on the bus, or at the bus stop.

When Sawyer asked the principal what Tom was expected to do if he was attacked first, the principal replied, "Turn the other cheek."

At those words, Sawyer launched from his seat and punched the principal in the face. "You turn the other cheek!" he yelled, grabbing Tom and bolting from the office.

Sawyer took Tom out of school, and he never finished the 10th grade.

For several more years, Tom numbed himself with marijuana and alcohol. He continued to work on construction crews or as a helper on the various labor crews Sawyer drifted to over the seasons.

When Tom's sister died at age fifteen from complications associated with her disability, Tom died emotionally. He deeply grieved the loss of his sister, because she had been the only true friend and confidant he ever had. By this time, Tom's mother had also become an alcoholic, which helped to numb her to the beatings Sawyer gave her when the two were drunk and quarrelsome.

Tom moved north to find a real job and escape the specter of his past. Soon after he left, he learned that Sawyer had died from undiagnosed lung cancer.

In the more than twenty years between the death of his sister and when Tom killed Gloria, Tom filled his life with every drug and drink available. He cycled through hallucinogens such as LSD, marijuana, and ecstasy. He became addicted to cocaine, until the cost of the drug and the risks of owing money to the wrong people scared him into quitting. He dabbled with high-purity heroin and opiates, during a time when younger, less-experienced addicts were dying from overdoses of these drugs.

He filled those years with women, too—sad women, who reminded him of his mother. These women were also alcoholics and drug addicts, and Tom wanted to save them from their unhappy, battered lives. Not surprisingly, he was unsuccessful, because he needed to be rescued himself. Eventually, he married a woman who was educated and had a successful career in business, despite also having a hidden, functional addiction to drugs and alcohol. Though Tom was attempting to start a new life, reminders from the past came back to haunt him. He received word that his mother had died of breast cancer; shortly after that, he received a letter from a Minnesota psychiatric asylum advising him that his father had died. The asylum reported that Tom's father died indigent and a ward of the state. They requested $500.00 in burial expenses.

Tom wrote a two-word expletive on the letter and mailed it back.

A few months later Tom went on disability and became addicted to pain killers. His wife left him and moved away.

Though Tom had experimented with so many drugs, alcohol was his substance of choice, always affordable, and always available. Tom's motto, his purpose in life, was to die drunk and happy.

But immediately after the accident, Tom sobered up. He arranged for counseling and began attending Alcoholics Anonymous meetings.

Five days after Gloria's death, Tom heard the sound of several cars pulling up in front of his trailer. As the car doors thudded closed, he peeled himself from the sofa to look outside. He figured it was the police coming for him. He was going to jail.

What Tom saw next was far more terrifying than the police. It was Gloria's family. Tom looked back at the sofa and remembered the neighbor had taken his gun. But it didn't matter, because he was resolved to die, and this would be the opportunity to end everything. He opened the screen door and stepped into the yard.

Gloria's sons approached Tom. They still wore their dress shirts and ties. An hour earlier, these sons, sons-in-law, and nephews had carried Gloria's casket to her grave and wept in a crowd as her funeral concluded and the grave was filled.

Tom held his arms out from his sides. He hung his head.

"Boys, I know why you are here. I don't blame you. I won't resist."

Tom braced for the end and hoped it would be one clean shot or one blow to the head, and he would feel nothing ever again.

They surrounded Tom, and he felt hands grabbing his arms and his back and his head. Someone, more than one, had his neck. He raised his eyes and looked into the face of Gloria's oldest son as he spoke.

"Our mother would want us to do this," he said. "She taught us to love God." He choked on the emotion in his words. "We came here to forgive you."

And they prayed.

After the prayer, one of the men said, "We forgive you, and God forgives you. But you know you need to answer for what you have done."

Tom felt the Holy Spirit come over him. He felt joyful, unlike any other time in his life. He knew God was real, and he finally understood forgiveness and grace.

On the day of his preliminary hearing Tom trembled. Because Tom planned to plead guilty, the hearing was waived. His attorney explained to the court that Tom planned to accept the sentence of the court.

In the parking lot, Tom thanked his attorney and then turned to me. He concluded that if it took this tragedy to save his life, then he had faith that there was a purpose left for him. As a sober man, with his AA group encouraging his relationship with God, he was willing to receive help from God and others, and he looked forward to helping others in need one day. With his hard-won sobriety, Tom's mind was functioning much more clearly, and that brought reality and purpose into sharper focus for him.

During his formal arraignment, Tom pled guilty, and a sentencing hearing was scheduled for the next month. Tom told the judge he was ready to go to prison that day; however, his attorney and the prosecutor contended that they had final details to resolve in the plea agreement.

Those final details became a testimony of God's grace toward Tom. Gloria's family had learned more about Tom's life history, including the ironic legacy of Tom's father killing the Vietnamese woman with the baby in her backpack. The similarity to Gloria carrying her grandson, his riding against her back on the motorcycle, was not lost on the family. They also learned that Tom's remorse and faith-driven sobriety were real miracles. They encouraged the prosecutor to agree to a sentence approximately half the time of what Tom deserved according to legal sentencing guidelines. He would spend less than five years in prison.

At sentencing, Gloria's family filled the courtroom. Tom stood next to his attorney, and I sat alone on the side. If there is one observation that I have made working with criminal offenders in court it is this: they are typically alone in the world. They often carry that loneliness with them for the duration of their prison sentence. They receive few, if any, visits, and the afternoon mail delivery can be an equally empty reminder that no one cared enough to write.

Gloria's oldest son spoke for the family. He read from a letter, and Tom had not heard his voice since the two were eye-to-eye in Tom's front yard nearly a year ago. The son managed to read most of the first page before he was overcome with choking emotion. Tom wept.

The judge asked for the letter, and he continued reading for the son. But even the judge had to pause at times to control his emotions and maintain the decorum of the court. As the judge read, the family wept with Tom.

When it was his turn for a statement, Tom gathered himself and turned to the family. He made eye contact with them, and spoke his confession and his promise to use the faith and the new chance in his life to do good for others as a way to honor what Gloria meant to them.

Tom was ordered to report to the county prison at the end of the week.

Outside the courtroom, Gloria's family hugged Tom, and he wept hard as our two groups entered the elevator together. A deputy sheriff recognized that we were together and became concerned because of the emotions and sobbing. I remember the last moments with Tom as we rode to the ground floor. Tom was caught in a family hug, and there was loud prayer; someone asked God to watch over Tom and to keep him well while he was in prison.

Outside the courthouse the family dispersed quietly. Tom shook our hands, lit a cigarette, and blended into the crowd with a grateful smile. I realized I had this knot inside my chest, and after quickly dismissing myself from the attorney, I got into my car before my own sobs exploded. There was nothing more to do but thank God for the opportunity to witness a miracle of grace. That was the last time I saw Tom.

I learned years later that Tom had survived prison well. While in prison, he was comforted by a visit from his wife, whom he had not seen or spoken to for years. During this time, the couple rekindled their love and reunited when Tom was paroled. Tom's healing began when he finally spoke out in prayer. Not only did he experience God's mercy, but he experienced the grace and forgiveness of those he had wronged, perhaps one of the most powerful, awe-inspiring encounters with Christ's love in people. He felt and heard the simple prayers of faithful people, and this encouraged his own humble prayers. Tom's future in a renewed marriage bond was also possible because his wife knew God's mercy, and her visit made the difference. Her visit was the fruit of a heart full of the love and grace of God.

CHAPTER 9
BEING BOLD

"And when they had prayed, the place in which they were gathered together was shaken, and they were all filled with the Holy Spirit and continued to speak the word of God with boldness."
—Acts 4:31

B eing a PI takes patience and courage, but it also takes boldness. To do my job well, I have to speak uncomfortable truths to others—about the offenders themselves, their friends and family members, and the consequences of the law. I also need to convince offenders that if they speak hard truths about themselves, it will serve them well in court. As a new Christian, confidently speaking truth took on a much greater meaning to me, but I sometimes felt inadequate compared to people who had been Christians for a much longer period of time. Like Gideon, I had to be bold when God told me to be, despite my insecurities.

Gideon was the lowest member of his family, from the weakest tribe, yet God called him to save Israel (Judges 6:15). Likewise, I was brand new in my relationship with God, and besides my mom, I had no Christian heritage to speak of. Yet God called me to advocate for a man who had gotten into some legal trouble. That man was Zach, and though God had directed me toward his case, nobody in Zach's family thought I could help him.

When I met Zach through his defense attorney, he was already a Christian. In our first meeting, I could see that Zach was a charismatic, friendly guy. In his late forties, Zach had been saved when he was young, and he loved to talk about God. He prayed openly for himself and others—that is, during his sober times.

Zach had been to rehab, and he candidly shared his history of drunkenness, then hitting rock bottom, then finding salvation. While in rehab, Zach taught younger men that alcohol was a deceptive problem-solver: when you were drunk, you felt like your problems didn't exist, but when you sobered up, they were still there waiting for you. Zach knew the Bible, taught Godly principles, and had a heart to help others.

Yet here he was, sitting in a conference room in a county jail, awaiting trial for assault with a deadly weapon.

I had researched Zach's criminal record before that first meeting, and I saw that his charges spanned more than twenty years. They were not clustered in concise time periods, as if he were having short stints of bad luck or brief patterns of self-destruction. Zach's whole adult life was scarred with alcohol and vehicular violations, along with various other criminal offenses.

Criminologists refer to this as a life course of criminal behavior.

Christians may refer to this as a life that is unhealed, maybe even unrepentant.

Despite his criminal record, Zach's love for God seemed sincere, and he truly wanted to be free of his addictions. I determined that something serious was driving his behavior, and I had to uncover it. If I did not, he would be facing five to ten years in state prison because his offense involved a firearm.

Though Zach spoke candidly to others about his drinking, he never talked about his arrest record. The family and friends I interviewed knew him as an alcoholic, but not as a criminal. For years, his Christian friends had prayed for God to heal him of alcoholism and stabilize his life. After decades of praying, that healing never occurred, and his friends' faith in his ability to turn back to God dwindled.

Additionally, several prominent preachers had attempted to minister to Zach, and though he would reform for a while, he would always relapse into his drunken, drugged lifestyle.

And then I came along, with my notebook, two ballpoint pens, and a list of questions.

What could I possibly do to help Zach in comparison to them?

Zach himself even helped to confirm my doubts.

"People like you, Brian. They don't have any doubt that you're good at what you do." He leaned forward over the conference table. "But they don't think you can help, because other people who have been in church a long time weren't able to help me."

I smiled at him, but I didn't believe it. God had provided so much direction to me in the previous week regarding how to help Zach, that I took these people's doubts and reservations as a spiritual attack from the enemy. It simply confirmed I was in the right place, doing the right thing.

If Zach had said that to me one week earlier, however, I would have agreed, closed my notebook, tucked my pen in my collar, made some small talk, and left. One week earlier, I felt that my spiritual abilities were limited by the short time I had known God, my inadequate knowledge of Scripture, and the faults and failures I saw in myself every day. But after praying earnestly and seeking God for help, I realized God was far bigger than my inadequacies. He could use anyone He chose to use, and

He would ultimately get the glory for completely healing Zach, not me. Now, following God's direction, I put my faith in God's abilities. I had no right to back out of Zach's case because others didn't think I could accomplish this task. Zach didn't want me to, I didn't want to, and I believed God didn't want me to.

So after Zach told me about his friends' and family's vote of no confidence, I opened my notebook, clicked the top of my pen, and began to ask questions.

I found that Zach wasn't just a heavy drinker: he was truly an alcoholic. He couldn't drink just one. He needed to drink all there was and then go get more. He became uninhibited when he drank, and this led to wild behavior like barroom brawls, and life-threatening situations like car wrecks.

One particularly bad accident landed Zach in the hospital, where he spent a month recovering from internal injuries and broken bones.

After this close call with death, Zach turned his life over to God. For the next six years, he pursued higher education as a means to a stable job. But on the road to a career as a teacher, he made a u-turn back toward a life of partying and illegal drugs. Friends and family were disappointed at this unexplained reversal, but they didn't know Zach had developed a second life as a cocaine addict and dealer.

His first arrest for DWI brought the addiction to light, and Zach agreed to drug rehab as a condition of his probation. Zach excelled on probation supervision. In the face of accountability and true consequences, he thrived and even felt happy.

Unfortunately, when he was off probation and no longer accountable, Zach would spiral back into substance abuse. His record included a half dozen more bouts with alcohol and substances, which included legal troubles, arrests, jail time, and probation. He would visit rehabs and go to counseling and AA meetings, but once clear of his sentence and the accountability of reporting to a probation officer every month, Zach returned to the bottle.

Zach even entered a faith-based rehab program—drawing on his love for God in stronger doses as his life course ebbed and flowed between drunkenness and sobriety. For a while, Zach benefited from the spiritual atmosphere and camaraderie of the program, eventually becoming a leader and role model to other men. But just as before, temptation found Zach, this time in the form of heroin, a drug he had not yet tried but always wanted to.

Within a few weeks of becoming addicted to heroin, Zach left the rehab. He hated himself for his hypocrisy and false Christianity. He returned home, and after a few more months of struggling with his cravings for heroin, Zach decided the lows were far worse than the pleasure of the highs. He gave up on heroin and nursed his physical withdrawal sickness with alcohol.

But he wasn't just using alcohol to medicate his withdrawal symptoms. He was still drinking for the same reason he had always used alcohol: to deaden the pain from memories, regrets, lost dreams, and his childhood. Zach said he dwelled on different, hurtful events from his past, and it felt to him like he was watching a room full of different movies all at the same time. Some screens were big and some were small. The volume of every movie was set at a different level that fluctuated dramatically and without his control. Zach's mind was a Cineplex of life experiences, and some of those events were not only distracting, they were downright crippling.

By using alcohol, Zach was able to slow down these thoughts and turn the mob of shouting voices into a quiet, single-file line. The first couple of drinks would corral his thoughts; the next several would subdue them; and the last few rounds would completely shut them out. Intoxication allowed Zach to switch off all of the movies in his mind. Not surprisingly, in this process, Zach developed a tolerance that required longer binges and the use of other drugs to achieve this mental silence.

He also developed more serious health problems.

Shortly after recovering from his heroin addiction, Zach was diagnosed with hepatitis C. Zach now saw his liver as a time bomb that would lead to death if his alcohol use did not end. But he admitted he was still cycling through those movies in his head, and only one thing helped him corral, subdue, and shut out those thoughts.

Instead of limiting his alcohol use, Zach evolved in it. He began to disappear for a week or two at a time to hide out in his family's old mountain cabin to drink. He would tell his family he was going out of town to work or visit friends, and then he would drive to the cabin so he could drink for days on end without putting himself or others in harm's way on the road. At the cabin, he drank vodka by the bottle, claiming to consume an average of two bottles a day. He sat on the couch, watched movies, and listened to rock music, from ballads to heavy metal.

Perhaps most disturbing—and most symbolic of the depths of Zach's alcoholism—was his "bib," a tunic-style apron he wore when he was drunk to protect his clothing from the vomit stains. He would drink until he became physically sick and completely fatigued, and then he would clean the cabin and return home. Though one or two thoughts still tugged at his emotions, Zach had drowned the majority of the bad memories with liquid poison.

Even though Zach used the cabin as a secure base for drinking, he began to bend his own rules about driving and periodically ventured out, sometimes for food, sometimes to replenish his vodka supply, and sometimes to sit on top of scenic vistas that overlooked the forest where he used to hunt and fish as a kid.

On one of those drunken drives, Zach veered off the road and became stuck in a ditch. It was early winter, and the soil was still soggy. Even in four-wheel drive, his truck needed some leverage to power all the wheels. In a farmhouse nearby, an old farmer heard Zach's truck tires whining against the rocks and mud. The farmer joined Zach, and together they kicked some stones under the wheels. He directed Zach to rock the vehicle back and forth, then reverse, then drive ahead. The farmer got behind the truck at an angle, and, despite his age, he was able to nudge the vehicle just enough so that Zach could drive onto the roadway.

Zach slid out of the driver's seat to survey the back of the truck for damage. When he was sure the truck was okay, he moved toward the ditch to inspect for property damage. As he did, Zach stumbled into the ditch and fell. He flopped and then stood up, unsteady. The world spun. Climbing out of the ditch, he looked at the farmer, who was kicking rocks and dirt from the road. Zach then turned toward his truck and swayed.

The farmer, immediately concerned, spoke to Zach with care.

"Son, I don't think you are all right to drive. Why don't you just sit down here on the bank for a little bit and rest?"

Zach tried to step into his truck, but the farmer put his firm hand on Zach's shoulder.

Spinning around, Zach batted his hand away. With surprising dexterity, he reached into the back of his waistband and drew out a handgun. He pointed the barrel at the farmer's face.

Several weeks later, when Zach and I met in the interview room at the county jail, he told me he had never been suicidal, but that since he was 11 years old, he didn't really care about living.

I asked Zach how he could know God and feel this way about life.

Yes, Zach said he knew God all his life. Yet he said he struggled with doubts and questions about why God would let him suffer so much if He really loved him. Though Zack loved God, He didn't trust Him to be good, and, deep down, he seemed to be angry at Him for something.

He admitted these doubts and questions related to other memories that tormented him.

Zach had been willing to tell me so much of his life story, but he still hadn't admitted what was driving a lifetime of self-destructive behavior. After years of being a PI, I've learned not to be too amazed at the depth of detail in an offender's story if he hasn't told me the hard truth about himself. I've learned that with almost every offender, there is always something more—some detail or event that clarifies or explains their criminal behavior. Though virtually Zach's entire story seemed like hard truth, it was apparent there was something more. That something was the catalyst for his pain, substance abuse, and disregard for life.

I told him as much. I told him I believed there was something more. Zach stared at me, silent.

I told him that his story seemed to revolve around some deep unhappiness from his childhood, and I explained that traumatic events in our childhood can have a deep impact on the way we live our lives as adults.

He sighed, as if he were about to relieve himself of a heavy weight. He stared at the table and chose his words carefully.

"There was this older boy in the neighborhood…"

I nodded. "Did he hurt you?"

"Yes."

"Sexually?"

His eyes brimmed with tears, but he didn't let them fall.

"Yes."

The boy who raped Zach lived in his neighborhood. They weren't friends, but he had seen him around. The first time Zach encountered the boy, he didn't see him, he heard him. While Zach and his friends were riding their bikes through the neighborhood, they heard his screams. As they rode by the boy's house, they could see the boy's father beating him mercilessly in the front yard. The boy kept trying to run, but his father grabbed him and beat him more. Eventually, the father dragged the boy into the house. Terrified, Zach and his friends watched until the shrill screams of the boy in the yard became muffled thuds and echoes inside the house.

It was in that house where the boy assaulted Zach less than a month later.

"When that old guy grabbed me by the shoulder, I could feel that kid's hands on me, and I just freaked," Zach said.

After the assault, Zach went home and told his parents.

They didn't believe him.

"They said, 'He's a good Christian boy! He would never do such a thing. Shame on you for lying like that about him.'" Zach's voice was a mix of heartbreak and sarcasm. "That's when I thought, if this is what life's like, it kinda sucks."

After that, Zach experienced years of insomnia and trouble at school. Compounding the shame and trauma, Zach saw the boy every Sunday at church for several more years; the boy would look at Zach but never talk to him. Zach was confused emotionally. He wanted to hurt the kid, but he also felt like crying. And he felt vulnerable.

He began carrying a knife.

As they grew older, the boy became a prominent adult in the community. While Zach had grown up to be a humiliated alcoholic with a life course of criminal behavior, his molester grew up to become a regular family guy with a job, a home, and nice cars. Zach hated him for what he had done and resented the injustice of his success. How could God bless someone like this when his life had been so cursed? Every time Zach would see this man in public—shopping at a store, eating at a restaurant, or attending church with his family—Zach burned with frustration and rage.

When he was twenty-one, he bought the handgun. Zach swore no man would ever touch him again.

And though he never experienced another assault, the nightmare of that one episode—the powerlessness and the humiliation—had been the shame that haunted Zach his whole life. This was the scene on the biggest screen of the movies that replayed in Zach's mind every drunken night, every drug-induced fix, every drunken binge at the cabin.

"What if I had run?" he asked with desperate regret. "What if I had been bigger and could have fought him? What if I had this gun—then what would he have done?"

Though Zach would never know what the boy would have done, he knew what the farmer did. With remarkable presence of mind, the farmer stepped to the side and grabbed Zach's gun. Zach kept his grip on the handle, and the two began to wrestle like snakes, twisting over one another for dominance. Though Zach was younger, the alcohol caused him to be clumsy and uncoordinated, making the fight more evenly matched. When the farmer realized he wasn't getting the gun from Zach, he decided to make it safe by firing into the ground. He straightened his arm, slid a finger into the trigger guard, and squeezed. One loud, smoky shot blasted into the mud.

They struggled more.

Inside the farmhouse, the farmer's wife heard the shot and ran to the door. She looked across the yard to the ditch and saw her husband struggling with a man. The gun fired a second time, then a third.

Her husband had repeatedly squeezed the trigger until the magazine was empty and the gun was no longer deadly.

She screamed and called 911.

Zach broke loose, leaving the farmer holding the empty gun. Panicked, Zach ran across the roadway to hide in the forest, eventually coming to a clearing. The farmer ran into his house, locked the door, and waited with his wife for the police.

When the police cars arrived, Zach was still standing in the clearing, looking around. He heard the sirens and the commotion. Soon after the police an ambulance arrived with siren blaring.

Zach was curious.

If Zach's story hadn't been so hurtful and humiliating, his accidental surrender would have been comical, like something in a movie. Still drunk, he emerged from the woods and walked up to a police officer, who was resting casually against the side of his cruiser. The officer was waiting for directions from his sergeant.

Zach asked, "What happened? What's going on?"

The officer, figuring Zach to be a crime scene spectator, responded to his question with indifference.

But when the farmer and his wife saw Zach, they screamed.

"Him! That's him!"

Immediately, the officers seized Zach and tossed him onto the hood of the cruiser. In seconds, he was handcuffed. They tore at his clothes and slapped his body, searching for weapons, and then stuffed him into the backseat of a cruiser. The door slammed behind him.

A short while later a police officer and a medic approached Zach. They checked him for injuries, and the officer wrapped a blanket around Zach's shoulders to keep him warm. It had been hours since he'd had a drink, and the descent to sobriety was making him ill. The bottle of vodka he had stashed in his truck was in the hands of the police now.

This would become the last time Zach drank alcohol.

He was charged with aggravated assault with a gun along with a host of other charges. Bail was set very high because he was seen as a danger to the community. Zach realized he had extinguished his grace with the probation system, and the judge now fully understood that Zach's alcoholism had advanced well beyond drunken driving.

The family pooled some money and hired a good defense attorney. But when I first spoke with him on the phone, his voice sounded bleak.

"He's looking at a minimum of five years because he used a gun," the attorney said. "And with his extensive criminal record, the judge doesn't have a lot of reasons to show mercy."

The attorney agreed that I could complete a mitigation profile in hopes the judge might recognize some of Zach's rehabilitative needs and his past success remaining sober while on probation supervision. But because Zach had failed to stay sober after probation times ended, the judge would most likely see him as a threat to society. And, of course, it was unlikely a judge would mitigate any crime that involved a gun.

Additionally, everyone, and I mean everyone, I interviewed—his family, his friends, his religious leaders—said it was hopeless. I heard the same message from different voices:

"He's been through so much; I doubt there is anything you could do."

"He really messed up this time, and no one can help him."

With patronizing smiles, they told me they appreciated my willingness to try, and I believed they did, but they didn't think my work would amount to anything.

One particular rationale resounded: "He went to a rehab that taught the Bible. He grew up in church. Men who've known the Bible a long time have tried and gotten nowhere with him…"

They would tick off the names of career religious leaders, some supposedly prominent leaders of mega-churches, whose names I didn't recognize—all of these men had known God for decades.

And all had failed to rehabilitate Zach.

Though none of these religious leaders knew me or actually asserted his longevity in God over me, the beliefs of Zach's friends and family played on my mind. For about a week, I felt discouraged, until I really thought about the tough cases and situations God had brought me through. I was convinced God had led me into this case and given me clear direction about how to proceed, and I felt like God wanted to do something both compassionate and miraculous for Zach. I decided that I would not be intimidated or discouraged by anyone, and I committed to fully rely on God for the outcome of Zach's case.

I boldly went to work, praying at the start of every meeting for God to be with Zach and me, and thanking God for being with us at the end.

Next to his parents, I was the only person Zach had ever told about his sexual assault. Sadly, I was the first to believe him. During every interview, I talked honestly with him and as a friend. I didn't judge him for being humiliated, and I didn't comment on the condition of his faith or his feelings toward God. I simply asked questions and listened.

During my second interview with Zach, he expressed his anger not just over the assault, but also over the boy's hypocrisy.

"That boy went to church, yet he did this to me," Zach said. "He hid behind that church, so no one would believe me. My parents believed him over me, because that boy went to church, and he acted like he knew God. I don't understand how God could let me suffer all this time."

"What would you do if that guy was here right now?" I asked.

"I'd kill him. I'd absolutely kill him for what I have gone through." I believed him.

Prison is no place for tears. Tears and emotions show weakness and if you are weak in prison, you are at risk. Zach hid his tears by holding perfectly still so they did not drip or trickle across his cheeks.

"One thing I always wanted was to be a father and to love my own kids," he said. "I had a vasectomy when I was in my twenties because I could not bring children into this world knowing something like this could happen to them."

Zach hadn't forgiven the boy and healed from this trauma because he had never shared this story with anyone who believed him and showed him grace. The trauma was sealed in a tomb inside Zach's heart. None of the men with decades of religious experience and good intentions ever asked Zach about his past or about his pain. Oddly, they couldn't see that the bad fruit in Zach's life had to be related to some bad roots. They were too blinded by the sins Zach was committing to consider that the catalyst for his behavior was a grievous sin that had been committed against him.

Instead of coming alongside Zach as brothers in the Lord, they had approached him as religious authorities, telling him right from wrong. Zach knew in his head what was right and what was wrong: he simply couldn't act on that knowledge because his heart was full of shame, wounds, and unforgiveness. Additionally, Zach wasn't convinced these religious men were safe enough to trust with such a painful memory— he was not convinced they wouldn't judge him for his response to the assault or insist that he immediately forgive the boy and "get over it." He also didn't feel safe enough to share with them his confusion and anger with God. Again, he was sure they would reprimand him for doubting God's goodness or blaming God for his trauma.

Somehow, in Zach's mind, these men "knew God" but they weren't safe.

God knew Zach needed something deeper than a religious leader telling him right from wrong: he needed a comforter, or what the New Testament, in the Greek language, calls a *Paraclete*—literally, one who pleads another's cause before a judge, someone called to the aid of another as a legal assistant. Both Jesus and the Holy Spirit are described with the word *parakletos* (John 14:26; 1 John 2:1), and both come alongside us to help us and advocate for us.

God had sent me to advocate for my brother.

I shared the story with Zach's attorney and he authorized the written social history and mitigation profile to be produced as fast as I could type.

When my profile was almost complete, I went to Zach's mother for some additional family history. She was cooperative but frankly amazed that I had spent so many hours with Zach and had obtained his assistance during several meetings at the prison.

Again, I felt that boldness from God. Gently, I asked her if Zach had ever spoken with her about an incident involving a neighbor boy when he was young.

Her mouth opened and tears poured from her eyes.

"Did that really happen to my son?" She hugged me and began to sob. "I never believed him."

God's compassion healed not only Zach's heart, but his mother's as well. The light of this hard truth gave her fresh perspective about her son's substance abuse and criminal behavior. They were both able to grieve the assault and come to terms with its impact on their family.

Beyond this emotional and relational healing, the judge granted Zach probation with time served. He did not go to state prison.

When the prosecutor gave the farmer my social history profile about Zach, the farmer was overwhelmed with empathy and encouraged the prosecutor to help Zach by getting him into the right treatment program to help him heal. Years of AA meetings and faith-based substance-abuse programs had only addressed the bad fruit in Zach's life; now Zach would be admitted into a treatment program for adult survivors of childhood sexual assault, who also had alcohol and drug addictions related to their trauma. In this program, the root causes of his drinking and drug use would finally be addressed, and true, lasting deliverance could finally take hold in his life.

And Zach was successful in his treatment program as well as the conditions of his probationary sentence. His understanding of God deepened, and his relationship with God is stronger and more stable than ever before. His family relationships have also become more honest and fulfilling, and he has developed a meaningful romantic relationship with a woman who is also a believer in God.

Zach is alive and sober today because of God's love. I'm thankful that God directed me to help him, despite the relatively short length of my walk with God and the challenges associated with Zach's case. This case built my faith and taught me that the miracles of salvation and healing in people's lives are possible through God's Spirit alone. It also taught me that no one is too far gone for God to reach them, even when it seems hopeless to others. God can use us to search for that one lost lamb. He did that for Zach, and He did this for me. I just had to be bold enough to take the first step.

CHAPTER 10
GOD FORGIVES GUILT

"Come now, let us reason together, says the LORD: though your sins are like scarlet, they shall be as white as snow; though they are red like crimson, they shall become like wool."
—Isaiah 1:18

Mark writes to me about once a month. In the first few years of his sentence, Mark continued to struggle with anger, and he tried to fill time by reading anything related to God and religion. Even though he had a relationship with God, and the threat of the death penalty was gone, he had marinated in his own anger for so long that the bitter flavor lingered in his soul.

Perhaps the greatest relief of Mark's anger, though, was his confession and closing statement, which included individual messages to his children. Under the guidance of his attorneys, I worked with Mark to prepare a concise and powerful statement. Mark spoke those words with much earnestness; his heart was in his voice, and no one—no witness, no prosecutor, no law enforcement officer—could negate his final words to the court.

Unfortunately, his children did not attend the sentencing, but his words to them were honest and sincere:

> *I can't expect to be forgiven for what I have done. I do not understand forgiveness because I have been an angry man for most of my life. I felt that I had a right to be angry and I lived much of my life believing that one wrong deserved another.*
>
> *I wish I could take back my anger, and I wish I could take back my actions. I failed to see that I had more to lose than my freedom. I felt I had already lost everything—I was wrong. In my narrow view, I saw my four children, who no longer knew me.*
>
> *Every day I think about my kids. Every day I want to write to my kids. Every day I think about the anger I had about losing my kids, and how I hid from my past, and I hid from being a father, because I couldn't handle the loss. I also lost the opportunity to be forgiven by my kids. I pray someday that they will forgive me.*
>
> *I have dreams that my kids will someday want to contact me, and that I can get to know them—even as a life inmate. I don't know how they can forgive me.*
>
> *I want to tell my daughters, I am sorry that I have failed you as a father. I hope you may someday let me talk to you. I'm proud that you have grown into fine women, and I hope you will always take care to find a life that is happy and to trust your love. But don't be involved with a man who is angry like I am. I want you to know I am sorry to have hurt your family, your mother, your brothers. I can remember our fun times as a family, and I am sorry for what I have done. When you are older, I pray for a chance to know you.*
>
> *I want to tell my sons that I am sorry to have left you. Do not become angry men. Do not let the anger I have cross into your life. I*

am confessing this to you to end this cycle. Be proud men and please be happy. I've lost those years. I've lost all years and I know the hurt you feel, because I grew up without a father. Break this cycle of anger. Love your family. Don't hold onto anger. Know that I want you to someday forgive me, and I pray to know you again.

Please forgive me.

Every professional in the courtroom was obviously moved. When a man bares his soul in such a remorseful way, it takes a calloused heart not to be sympathetic. This was one of the few situations in which I've been involved that the gravity of the confession brought a true closure for the justice system. This does not mean the family of Mark's victim does not forever grieve; it simply means that in respect to the justice system, this ending was satisfactory.

The prosecutor did not make a speech. He did not lambaste Mark with humiliation and more shame. He was dignified.

The judge expressed his thankfulness that Mark held himself accountable for his crime and provided a careful and sincere statement. He sentenced Mark to life in prison and wished him luck.

In one way, criminal court is like a church wedding: when you enter the courtroom, it's important to sit in the correct place. There is the prosecution's side, and there is the defendant's side. Sadly, the defendant's side of the courtroom is usually empty. Although Mark's oldest brother, his mother, and his two sisters provided extensive support to the social history part of my investigation, they were absent at sentencing. But Mark's closest lifelong friend, his brother Eddie, did show up. It was a strange occurrence.

I had never met Eddie, although I made significant steps to find him. Eddie had eluded me, as he had eluded a number of police officers, who were hunting him for more information on the case. The police had ambushed Eddie on the morning of Mark's arrest.

They had search warrants and raided his rented apartment. They also had an arrest warrant. They convinced Eddie to give up Mark's hiding spot with the threat of charging Eddie with conspiracy or obstruction of justice.

Eddie was street-smart with the cops, but he wasn't stupid. Mark had already admitted the crime to his brother, and Eddie was in shock. He knew how deeply Mark loved his children, but he never thought Mark would go this far. Because Eddie was concerned Mark might commit suicide, he willingly gave up Mark's hiding spot at a cabin several miles outside the city. Mark's suicide was a loss Eddie could not endure.

When I arrived at the courthouse, Mark was in a conference room with one attorney, while Eddie was in another conference room with another attorney on Mark's legal team. I introduced myself to Eddie and listened while Eddie unraveled.

He was emotional. Desperate. He insisted that Mark was making a mistake by pleading guilty. His street code told him that Mark needed to fight the charges and that the death penalty didn't matter. I explained to Eddie how this was Mark's decision, and that everyone was following Mark's wishes. I told Eddie that if he wanted to be involved in the case, he shouldn't have evaded me for so many months. Eddie explained that by evading me, he was also evading the police, who would undo all the good I had done for Mark.

I asked Eddie if he had any active warrants for his arrest—for anything.

"I don't know."

"How can you not know if you don't have any warrants?"

Eddie didn't answer.

I assumed he did.

We kept Eddie concealed in the conference room until the judge was ready for the sentencing hearing to begin, then Eddie and I took a seat behind the defense table. Mark had a chance to see his brother for the first time since his arrest, and they spoke a few words. Their love was clear. Eddie sobbed and held his face in his hat.

During the hearing, Mark's legal team feared Eddie would erupt with an outburst that would dilute the power of Mark's sincerity during his final statement. My job was to watch Eddie and contain him if necessary. He would cry and lift his head and shoulders abruptly to catch a glimpse of who was speaking or to react to what was said. Eddie wanted to speak, but my hand on his shoulder kept him seated. Though a middle-aged man, Eddie was all muscle, and when he occasionally lunged and lurched, it was like holding a wolf on a thin leash. But I didn't just need to contain Eddie. I needed to talk to him. Even though Mark was on his way to a life sentence, Eddie was the missing piece. His knowledge of Mark would bring clarity to the vague spots in Mark's social history profile. Eddie's familiarity with Mark's life would finish the work.

I prayed for Mark as he spoke. I prayed for Eddie as Mark spoke. Eddie tensed and tightened his shoulders and arms, then slumped with sobs. At the end, deputies re-cuffed Mark and escorted him out of the courtroom. I stood to speak to Mark as he passed by, but when I turned back toward Eddie, I saw that Eddie had vanished.

I had to find him.

The deputies in the hallway were little help. They were friendly, but even though this was the only major case in court that day, none of them recalled seeing Eddie leave the courthouse. I figured his head start couldn't have been that long. I ran outside, and another deputy on the steps remembered seeing a guy who fit Eddie's description. He was pedaling away on a bicycle.

Eddie lived almost 30 miles from the courthouse. Initially, I was shocked at the distance he had ridden, but remembering Eddie's fitness level, it wasn't impossible. My challenge now was to figure out which way he had ridden. Several main roads and numerous back roads led out of the city. Given the number of possibilities, I had no choice but to canvass the area and find him.

The best method I've found to canvass for a mobile subject is to take the most obvious direction of travel and then drive the maximum distance he could get based on the time he started traveling. By doing this, I've often found the person while en route. Of course, Eddie was on a bike, so the obvious direction of travel to me could be entirely different to him. He could be just around the corner. Or he could stop at a bar. What if someone he knew picked him up in a car? What if he had a weapon and planned to attempt to free Mark from the deputies? My imagination swirled as I drove.

I weaved my truck up and down country highways and major back roads that ran between the courthouse and the city. Within a few hours, I had clocked almost 100 miles. It was tedious and Eddie was nowhere.

What if the cops had picked him up on some warrant?

I drove back to a main country highway and parked near an intersection about 15 miles from the city. I had burned my afternoon searching for this guy on a bike with no real clue regarding direction of travel. I had run mileage without any success. And I had done all of this without seeking God's direction. As I sat there, I realized I had not prayed during this search. I had become so caught up in the driving that I completely forgot to ask God for help. God had directed so much of Mark's case, and I felt dumb that I had not asked for his direction first.

My prayer was simple: "God, you know how important Eddie is to me. You know this man is hurting for his brother. If you want me to find Eddie, please put him before me. Please lead me to find Eddie."

For me, a lot of trust goes into a prayer like this. I wanted desperately to find Eddie, but I was really asking God to give me peace with whatever happened, especially if I didn't find him.

I started the truck again and turned onto the highway toward the city. Before I had even accelerated to the speed limit of the road, there was Eddie cresting the top of a hill, pedaling furiously.

Smiling and shouting thanks to God, I drove past Eddie and pulled off at a shale pit to wait for him. I grabbed a bottle of cold water from my cooler and leaned against the back of the truck.

Eddie wasn't nearly as happy to see me.

He cursed.

"Why do I want to talk to you?"

I offered him the bottle of water and he cursed again.

"Why would I take a drink from you?"

Eddie then unleashed his anger, telling me without any prompting the story of their lives. Their father had left them. They raised themselves. Mark had the best life and a dream family. That man came at Mark's wife and pursued her. He was the one who did wrong, not Mark. Mark was defending his family. Mark's kids loved him and wanted him back, and now they couldn't see him because of their mother and what Mark did.

People will rubberneck at just about anything, and I remember the cars that would slow down to watch Eddie, who was in my face, pointing at me and waving his arms madly.

I just stood there and nodded.

Occasionally, when a car would slow down and look concerned enough to stop and get involved, I'd smile at Eddie with an open-mouthed grin, almost like I was laughing. This drove Eddie wild with fury, but it kept the onlookers moving along. As he continued to shout his story and scream profanity, he also sobbed. I prayed that no matter how many cars drove past, and how crazy or out of control the scene appeared, no one would call the police and no random patrol car would happen along.

After thirty minutes of rage and heartbreak, Eddie asked me if he could "really" have a bottle of water.

We put his bike in the back of my truck and headed toward the city. Eddie had quit cursing and enjoyed the cold water and air conditioning.

He told me that on several occasions after Mark's arrest, he rode his bike to visit Mark's children. He made sure that he visited the kids when their mother was working and they were home alone.

"Mark needs to know that his kids still love him, but they're in a difficult spot because they need their mother, too," Eddie said. "They cry for Mark. When they grow up and are on their own, I'm pretty sure they will come around."

When Mark got through the Department of Corrections' classification process and he was assigned a permanent prison location, I wrote to him to explain my abrupt disappearance from the courtroom and subsequent pursuit of Eddie. Most importantly, I told Mark about Eddie's visits to his kids. I told Mark how much his children still loved him.

When Mark read this, he wrote later, a profound hope exploded in his heart, and his faith in God blossomed along with the knowledge of his children's love.

Mark occupied his prison days by reading the Bible, and he collected other references about biblical history and various religions and doctrines. He undertook several Scriptural study courses and outlined the Bible according to various themes.

"God gave us only one book," he told me during a visit. "It should take the average man about two weeks to read it cover to cover. All I know is that if I'm called to the Kingdom, and God asks me how I spent life, I want to have something to talk to him about."

A few years after I turned my life to God, I was baptized. The date of my baptism was memorable for a couple of reasons. First, it was the same date that my dad had died a few years earlier. I had forgiven him, and for me, my baptism highlighted the forgiveness in my heart toward him. Second, the same afternoon I was baptized, I got a message from Mark's sister.

She had gone to visit Mark at the prison. This was the first time she had seen Mark since he had been transferred to his permanent location.

Mark's oldest son accompanied her.

Mark and his son had not seen each other in over ten years. His son's visit—their reunion—brought truth to Eddie's prediction. His son's desire to see his dad was the beginning of the emotional healing and forgiveness from his children that Mark longed for.

Though Mark prays and studies the Scriptures, he still experiences moments of stress and anxiety within the prison. Except for his small work crew, he keeps to himself to avoid trouble. He has also found a few friends who, like him, are lifers with relationships with God. They give each other support and pray for peace in each other's hearts.

Mark has good days and bad days. He believes God forgives and makes forgiveness possible, but he had struggled with one question that he finally asked me during a visit a few days before Christmas.

"If I died and went to Heaven, do you think he would be there? Would he forgive me for killing him?"

I was startled by his question. Unlike some of the other men in these stories, Mark had not experienced the forgiveness of his victim's family. He didn't know what it was like for his victim's friends or family members to hug him or put their hands on his shoulders and pray for him. In my cases, I've found that such human compassion helps to make God's forgiveness more perceptible to the offender. It brings God's grace down to earth in a way that helps to release offenders from guilt and shame. Unfortunately, in regard to the victim and his family, Mark was alone in his guilt.

As a young Christian, I had never been asked such a difficult question. How could I know this truth? What would God say? What if I tell Mark something that goes against the Scriptures? I had no idea how to respond to Mark, but thankfully God's Spirit was there to help me with my words.

I told Mark that what he had done was wrong, but rather than worry if his victim would forgive him, he should focus on his own relationship with God and let God, who is both just and merciful, determine the eternity of his victim. I also told him to pray for his victim's family and friends, that they would heal emotionally and find God in the pain of losing their friend and relative.

Though it is powerful and healing when the victims' families forgive the offender, such mercy may not occur. In these instances, offenders must rely on the truth of God's grace, which can be found in the Word of God. No amount of human forgiveness is more reliable than God's promises of forgiveness in the Bible. His Word is the truest foundation for our salvation and eternity. Thankfully, Mark knew the Bible well and was able to find peace in its passages about grace, mercy, and eternity in Heaven.

I had been used to answering tough legal questions, but Mark's tough spiritual question helped me to know what to anticipate when I visit someone in prison. His question also revealed the issues that many offenders ponder while in prison. They are looking for truth and wisdom that will change their perspective, and a wise response to a haunting question could change their faith forever. Similarly, those unanswered questions make an already lonely and desperate place more painful. Our visits, such as my visit to Mark before Christmas, and our willingness to speak God's wisdom from his Word can bring healing and closure to an inmate's lingering guilt.

Chapter 11

FORGIVENESS IS FREEDOM

"Now the Lord is the Spirit, and where the Spirit of the Lord is, there is freedom."

—2 Corinthians 3:17

F or most of my life, I knew nothing about my father's family. I didn't know how big his family was or who my cousins were, and I could only faintly recall seeing some of his relatives at a few funerals. One of those funerals was my Aunt Helen's. I didn't know her at all, but at age twenty-one, I was enlisted as a pall bearer. She had died during a particularly harsh rural Pennsylvania winter, and on the day of her funeral, the air was bitterly cold and furiously windy.

During his sermon, the old country preacher said something about Helen's soul being free—and then *bang!* The double doors of the church flew open in a gust of wind, as if Aunt Helen's soul had jumped out of her casket and bolted for the doors, yelling "Free at last!" The effect couldn't have been better timed. I knew it was the air pressure from the nor'easter, but I was not above being awakened spiritually—although it was temporary.

Many years later, I got to know Aunt Helen's son, Landon. We met by chance when he recognized me at a diner in my hometown. In that brief conversation, Landon told me three things: We aren't getting any younger. Cousins are all that are left in our family. It would be good to catch up. He gave me his phone number on a napkin, and then we each ate breakfast with our respective friends.

Though I didn't know my dad's side of the family, getting to know Landon would be a step to the truth. I called him, and a week later I met Landon at his house with our wives.

I told Landon I hoped he could fill in the gaps. Confused, Landon asked about my dad, and I confessed that he had abused me when I was young. Though I had a lot of anxiety about telling others this truth, it was liberating. Landon's response was a mix of surprise and compassion. I also told him about my wife and how we met, fell in love, and married; I told him about my salvation and relationship with God; and I told him about the freedom I received when I forgave me father for his abuse. I credited God with my ability to forgive.

Then Landon revealed my father's legacy to me.

My father's mother had been raised in an abusive family. When she married my grandfather and had eight kids, she dominated their farmhouse with the same physical brutality she had experienced growing up. My grandfather, on the other hand, was a simple, kindhearted man, who endured her violence until he could take no more. Grandpa Baker, finally sick of his wife's verbal abuse and beatings, quit his job as a janitor at the neighborhood school, packed his things, and landed unexpectedly on my uncle's doorstep in California, where he got a job in a factory and started a new life. Perhaps Grandpa thought he could leave his wife because seven of his children were already out of the house—all of his children, that is, except my dad.

My father, the baby of their family, was eight years younger than his next oldest sibling. He was fourteen years old when his father moved to California, and the rest of his brothers and sisters had already moved out of the house and started families of their own. No one was left to save my dad from his mother's cruelty. His father had abandoned him, and he had to weather her rage alone. To make matters worse, after her husband left, my grandmother had no income and was forced to receive welfare assistance.

Several years later, Grandpa Baker returned to Pennsylvania, got a small camper next to a creek, and hung a shingle that read "Baker Park." He spent the rest of his days feeding the animals and visiting relatives—everyone but my dad. My dad forever hated his father for leaving him alone with such an abusive woman. When Grandpa Baker died, I was a couple of months old, and he had only met me one time.

I never heard my dad talk about Grandpa Baker. Not once.

As if to punctuate Landon's account, my clearest memory of Grandma Baker is dinner at a local diner, where she stole the salt and pepper shakers, the glass cylinder of white sugar, and the chrome napkin dispenser, all of which my dad had to pay for. What had seemed like a funny scene to me as a little kid was just one episode in a lifetime of her habitual shoplifting—yet another humiliation to my dad.

A couple of years later, she died alone in a nursing home. Though she had passed on, my father's anger and abuse did not. The two primary sources of his rage, his mom and his dad, were both gone, but his unforgiveness and shame continued to fuel his hateful treatment of me.

As Landon went on to fill in the details of my father's lonely, battered, and rejected life, I listened, stunned.

Until then, I had no idea my father had suffered so much, and that his own suffering and shame had fueled the rage he took out on me. My father's pretext had been airtight, iron-clad. He hadn't let anyone near his secret shame—his humiliation at suffering physical abuse from his mother and being abandoned by his father.

Though Landon's story didn't excuse my father's behavior, it did provide an explanation. I had finally heard the truth I needed to understand why my dad had abused me. Though I had forgiven my dad based on God's grace and forgiveness toward me, God had then provided a window into my dad's life, so I could know, once and for all, that I wasn't responsible for his cruelty. I wasn't a failure as a son or unlovable. I was the victim of an abusive man, who himself had been an abuse victim. For the first time in my life, I not only felt forgiveness toward my father, but sympathy as well.

Landon's story helped to mitigate the circumstances surrounding my physical abuse. The information he shared about my dad brought healing and closure to a very long, painful chapter of my life. From this experience, I gained a more personal understanding of how my mitigation profiles could help to heal the emotional wounds suffered by crime victims and their family and friends. After hearing Landon's profile of my father, I could personally testify that gaining an understanding of the offender's circumstances can lead to empathy, compassion, and deeper forgiveness.

In addition to better understanding my dad now, though, my friendship with Landon also offered me the opportunity to meet more cousins. A bare side of my family tree was beginning to bloom. Cousins who thought I was aloof or snobby learned that my dad had intentionally alienated my mom and me from the rest of the family. While my dad had cloistered himself away from bad memories, he had isolated me as well, and even told lies about me to inflate his own wounded ego. But instead of inflaming my anger, as they would have in the past, these lies only increased my sympathy for him. His attempt to smear my reputation and belittle me now appeared more sad and pathetic than offensive and rage-inducing.

Another cousin I met through Landon was Linda. She shared deep family history with me and provided information that helped to further clarify my father's behavior and his lack of relationship with other family members.

Linda is also a lifer in a Florida women's prison. In 2003, she was arrested for the murder of her estranged husband. Her case lingered for several years until it went to a jury trial and she was convicted. I had never met Linda, but when her name came up during a conversation among cousins, I felt like I was missing something in my life. Somehow, I knew I needed to be introduced to her.

Our introduction was a step of faith. I went online to the inmate locator system (every prison has one) and found the mailing address for her institution and her inmate number. I didn't beat around the bush in my letter: I got straight to the truth of who I am, what I know about our family, and what God has done in my life. Linda had been a Christian most of her life, and prison has strengthened her walk with God substantially. She was excited to hear from me and she was eager for correspondence and visits.

My visits with Linda were mutually blessed. As she came to know me, she learned more about my dad, who was her uncle. We talked about his motives behind purposefully and maliciously estranging our family from hers. These conversations helped her to forgive my dad and bring healing to painful family memories.

Linda had a remarkable understanding for the importance of knowing your family legacy. She shared with me the trauma she had experienced growing up and this colored the circumstances that led to her own incarceration. We are undoubtedly products of our childhood experiences, and Linda shared with me the imperfections of her past that had formed her perspectives.

When Linda committed her crime, she had walked with God for many years. She had been married for over twenty years to a wonderful man who loved God and had served as the pastor for a small church. When they moved to Florida, they served together as the couples' ministers for a large church. Then her husband died of cancer, and Linda grieved deeply, clinging to God and her friends for survival.

Then a new man showed up in church. He was single and charming. Some of Linda's friends suggested they date—that this man may help Linda get back into life and recover from the loneliness and isolation she felt. Reluctantly, she went along with the introduction, and after a quick courtship, she married this man.

In her grief, coupled with her friends' haste in pushing her into a new relationship, Linda neglected to seek God for true discernment. She ignored the red flags and gut feelings that told her marriage to this man was a bad idea. Her well-intentioned friends wanted her to be happy, and this nice, Christian man showered her with kindness and attention. How could it be wrong, they wondered? In their minds, God surely sent him to Linda to ease her sorrow.

But they were wrong.

Though this man "talked the talk," he was not what he appeared to be.

His violent abuse tore open emotional scars that God had healed from her past. She had gone from living with a kind, gentle, Godly husband to being married to a vicious, sadistic, evil man. His battering and intimidation robbed her of the peace she had grown accustomed to and replaced it with anxiety and torment.

Her marriage to this man was a mistake she could not live with for the rest of her life.

Though she was convicted, she prays with devotion to God and spreads the Gospel to other inmates. Her friends remain committed and visit her regularly. She writes and calls from prison, and her example of faith is stronger than many Christians I know who churn through the same routine week after week. When I visit Linda, I see physical weariness, but I also see the twinkle of joy in her eye that is unmistakably God's Spirit when she smiles, grabs my hands to pray, cries, and thanks God for the blessings He brings to our lives.

Linda knows that God is a loving and forgiving Father. She knows the true story of Jesus. God's enduring love is the one truth that keeps her situation from being a hell on earth.

For me, visiting Linda is a blessing. Knowing her is among the greatest experiences I've had through God. And my relationship with her is possible only through forgiveness.

If I hadn't forgiven my father, I would never have been willing to speak with Landon; I wouldn't have wanted anything to do with my father's family. By speaking with Landon, I learned so much about my father and my cousins, including Linda. Because God had transformed my heart, I was able to be empathetic and compassionate to Linda, rather than judgmental. And my relationship with Linda has shown me what true Christianity is all about. In her most desperate times, behind bars for life, she still sings praises to God, reads His Word, and testifies of His goodness to others. She believes in his mercy and forgiveness, and she anticipates seeing Him in Heaven one day.

Though she also anticipates spending the rest of her life in prison, she is free in her spirit, because God's Spirit lives within her. I'm blessed to write to her, visit her, and pray with her. Though I am on the outside ministering to her behind bars, her letters always minister to me, too.

God has freed us, and we love to share that freedom with each other and anyone God brings into our lives.

CHAPTER 12
YOU VISITED ME

"And the King will answer them, 'Truly, I say to you, as you did it to one of the least of these my brothers, you did it to me.'"
—Matthew 25:40

P rison is lonely and desperate. For those of us who are friends or family of inmates, we can never fully understand the weight of a prison sentence, whether it is a finite sentence, life, or the death penalty. We can never fully understand the weight on a person's conscience who has committed a crime, particularly an offense such as homicide or drunken driving that has taken a human life. And we can never fully understand the pain offenders feel as they stare at the empty side of a courtroom, watch the mail cart pass by without a letter, or see other inmates visit with loved ones while they are alone. This isolation means they are forgotten, and the messages sent by our absence are more haunting than the loneliness: you are no longer important; we are humiliated by what you did; we do not forgive you; we want nothing to do with you; we are pretending you don't exist. These messages are laced with contempt, which can be distancing and dehumanizing, and add to the shame so many offenders already feel.

Offenders may continue to uphold a tough pretext, especially in prison where displays of weakness can prove dangerous. They may seem indifferent to our lack of connection to them, but inside they long for human relationship.

I have never met a prisoner who did not want a friend.

When I visit offenders in prison, I take a few moments to talk to them and although they know I can't help them with a grievance or a problem or stress point that is affecting them inside the block, they are relieved to have someone safe they can vent to. I also get a lot of letters that include the same venting… being heard helps relieve the pressure.

I don't go in with an agenda and I don't preach… I listen.

I'm not in there for myself. I'm there to do a job, and part of that job is to hold space and to listen: about anything and everything sometimes. When our conversations go off of the legal matter or the topic of investigation into other subjects, it's not about me. The solutions to many of the offenders' problems are found in God, and if I have that little bit of wisdom to encourage someone about God's love, I will do so. It's about God and what God wants to do for that offender. Gideon needed to believe that God could use him despite his shortcomings (Judges 6:15), and Paul considered all of his former religious qualifications a loss compared to knowing Christ (Philippians 3:8). I try to follow God's direction, reveal God's love to the inmate through words and actions, and give God the glory for the outcome.

With that in mind, I've noticed some patterns in the lives of offenders I've helped to defend over the years, and they are highlighted throughout these stories, including my own. Understanding these patterns can help us to express God's love in the most effective way possible.

Every offender I've worked with, and many people I've known who are not criminal offenders, live behind some form of a pretext. For my father and me, it was the pretext of being successful career and family men. Joe hid his fragility and sadness behind his muscular physique and dogged pursuit of heroic work in law enforcement. Zach's wide-grinned, charismatic personality shielded others from his secret shame. Tom attempted to appear strong enough to rescue others, particularly women, though he needed to be rescued himself. And Mark hid his shame of abandonment by working hard and building a family of his own. Even Linda hid her grief over the death of her beloved husband beneath the guise of a good, Christian woman—appearing full of faith and accepting of God's will when she was actually deeply confused and emotionally devastated.

Such pretenses can be confusing if we take them at face value. Because they often are an effective coping strategy for navigating a world that seems uncertain at best and dangerous at worst, it's easy to believe we are connecting with the real offender when we are actually interacting with his or her well-constructed persona.

And offenders often construct pretexts for this reason: they are hiding painful events in their past from the prying, judgmental, or condemning view of others. Every offender I have worked with has experienced circumstances, particularly in their childhood, that have caused a great deal of shame and heartache. In the stories here, we've seen bullying, abuse, abandonment, disappointment, trauma, sexual assault, divorce, rejection, and humiliation as some of the shaming events offenders have attempted to cover up. Because such shame is kept secret, it remains an open wound in the soul and infects a person emotionally until it festers into other coping strategies, such as substance abuse and criminal behavior.

Additionally, since substance abuse and criminal behavior are visible to society, we clearly see the sins the offenders commit, rather than the sins committed against them that have catalyzed their criminal behavior. As a result, we can sometimes be quick to condemn them for their actions. This is particularly true of Christian offenders, like Zach and Linda, who "should know better." We often focus on the bad fruit in their lives—the self-destructive, criminal behavior—and we forget to check the metaphorical soil in which they are planted to determine the root problems that have led to the behavior. As Christians, we mistakenly stop at being fruit inspectors when we need to continue to be root inspectors (Matthew 13:1-23). By seeking to understand the past events in an offender's life, not only do we better understand their criminal choices, but we also open the door for compassion, empathy, mercy, and grace.

I see my mitigation profiles as a legal approach to "root inspection," in which I dig deep into the offenders' lives to discover past events that may have motivated their criminal behavior. In many cases, when legal professionals, the victims, or their families read the profiles, a desire to show mercy to the offender results. Because they've gained a deeper understanding of the offender at the root level, they better understand why the offender acted out criminally. As a result, the victims and their families often feel compassion for the offender and want to see him rehabilitated, if possible, or receive a reduced prison sentence, if applicable to the charges.

This process was evident in Zach's case. When the prosecutor shared my mitigation profile with the farmer, he felt compassion for Zach and wanted to ensure he received the proper treatment related to adult survivors of childhood sexual abuse so Zach could heal emotionally. For Tom and Joe, however, a mitigation profile wasn't the means of sharing their stories. In both cases, community members and friends shared these offenders' back stories with their victims' families. After hearing the painful events in both men's lives, the families approached the prosecutors and requested reduced sentences.

In these cases, understanding the offenders at a deep level was the gateway to the families' willingness to show mercy and forgiveness.

In addition to pretexts used to cover shaming past circumstances, two other important elements of the pattern I've encountered with offenders are the need to confess the hard truths of those circumstances and to forgive those who hurt them. For offenders to reach this point, however, they need to feel safe enough to let down their pretexts.

Because we cannot control when people will peel away their pretexts to reveal their authentic selves, we need to be aware of these hiding strategies and the reasons for them, and then create the safest relational environment possible for an offender to be honest and vulnerable.

Most of us know people who are perceived as judgmental and willing to condemn others, and they are not likely to be chosen as confidants. Likewise, people who are perceived as gossips with the potential to spread shaming information are often not trusted, either. From an offender's perspective, to reveal humiliating past events to such people is equal to asking that more shame be heaped upon him.

Not surprisingly, people will test a person by floating trial balloons in conversation, such as, "I had a friend who stole jewelry from a roommate one time," or "A friend of mine was raped as a little kid," to gauge the listener's response. The more condemning the response, the less safe the listener will seem; conversely, the more gracious and compassionate the response, the safer the listener will appear.

It's obvious, then, that people who are perceived as helpful are often chosen as confidants. This is where experience and empathy are essential. If we come alongside offenders as brothers and sisters rather than as parents or religious authorities—if we present ourselves as helpers rather than "know-it-alls"—there is a better chance the offender will be more comfortable—even in his or her vulnerability—and less likely to feel the need for a pretext. And we do not need to be official religious leaders with titles to accidentally present ourselves as religious authorities:

if we come across as knowing everything there is to know about the Bible, as having overcome all sin and temptation, and as having all the answers to life's mysteries, we are well on our way to developing a one-up, one-down relationship with the offender. This approach can create a lot of emotional distance and uncertainty in the relationship, and we can become like the "miserable comforters" who could not refresh Job's spirit or console him in his time of need (Job 16:2).

Related to this, most offenders I know have had troubled and often traumatic relationships with their fathers. In these stories, several of the men had been abandoned or abused by a father or step-father. These painful past experiences make it hard for them to connect with and trust father figures, especially God the Father. If we are men ministering to offenders, and we present ourselves as stern, all-knowing, religious father figures, we have the potential to alienate and belittle the offender, causing further shame, hurt, and distance.

But when we are open about our own past experiences, flaws, and sins—if we live out humility and repentance rather than the appearance of sinless perfection—offenders not only realize that we are fallible humans, just like them, but they also recognize that *we know* we are fallible humans. The Bible says that if we say we have no sin, we are deceiving ourselves (1 John 1:8). Sinless perfection is not possible this side of heaven, but humility and repentance are. And since humble repentance is a component of Biblical salvation, showing that we are willing to admit our wrongdoings before God and ask for forgiveness can be a more powerful witness than seeming to have all the answers.

This means we need to be comfortable telling our own stories of salvation, including the parts that are less than flattering and even shaming. It was very hard for me to talk about the abuse I had suffered growing up, even after I was born again. I felt embarrassed that someone, who was supposed to love me, had beaten me up for years, and I thought people would think I was weak if they knew the truth about how my father treated me. When I met with my cousin Landon in his home, I was embarrassed even then to tell my story, but I am so glad I did. Not only did it clear up misconceptions in his mind about me, but it also opened the door for him to tell me about my father's past. Additionally, he felt more comfortable opening up to me about his life. I've shared my story with many offenders, and though my story is never exactly the same as theirs, they know that I understand pain, rejection, isolation, and wrong choices.

Over the years, it has gotten easier to share my story—to the point I'm now writing a book about it! As Christians, we need to reflect on all parts of our stories, and if there are memories that still cause pain and shame, we need to take those to God for healing. We also need to look for areas in our lives where we may need to forgive those who hurt us. At a very early point in my walk with God, I was eager to share the good news of Jesus with others, but I still needed to forgive my father for his abuse. If I hadn't obeyed God and forgiven him, I would have missed tremendous blessings that have come through my dad's side of the family, particularly through Landon and Linda. My ministry to others wouldn't be as effective and meaningful, either.

As we've seen in these stories, forgiveness brings healing and closure, while ushering in mercy and grace.

To better understand this, consider the parable of the Good Samaritan (Luke 10: 25-37). Two religious leaders showed no love to a Jewish man left for dead on the road, but one outcast Samaritan not only showed love, he showed lavish love. He came alongside the man, bound his wounds, poured oil and wine on them, put him on his beast, got a room for him at an inn, and stayed with him all night. In Jesus' story, being a neighbor had nothing to do with knowing someone, living near that person, or even liking him. The Jews and Samaritans couldn't have been more different, distant, or disdainful to each other. Instead, to Jesus, being someone's neighbor was defined through the expression of costly, sacrificial love.

In this parable, The Greek word for the man's wounds is *trauma* (v. 34). According to the original language, this man had suffered a traumatic beating. His assailants had stripped off his clothes and beaten him until he was half-dead. The word translated "wounded" (v. 30) is the Greek word *plēgē*—the same word used to describe whippings that law-breakers would receive (e.g., Acts 16:23; 2 Corinthians 6:5). When the Samaritan found this man, his wounds were open and bleeding, and he was completely exhausted.

Unlike the religious leaders, the Samaritan attempted to alleviate the trauma this man had endured. In Bible times, olive oil was used to soften the flesh and soothe the pain of a wound, while wine was used as an antiseptic to kill the bacteria—something like an ancient first-aid kit. He applied these to the man's wounds and bandaged them to prevent further infection.

The function of oil and wine in the open wounds sounds a lot like the effect of grace and truth in a hurting, sin-sick soul. If churches are like hospitals for the spiritually unwell, a prison can be like a morgue for the spiritually dead. Similar to Jesus' ministry on earth, when offenders can hear the word and feel it in our kindness and attention, we help to heal the brokenhearted and bind their wounds (Luke 4:18).

I believe the story of the Good Samaritan perfectly captures what it means to have compassion on an offender and do everything in our power to alleviate his suffering and the suffering of his friends and family members. Metaphorically, the Samaritan recognized the man's trauma, brought grace and truth to him, brought him to a secure place, and provided for his healing needs. To do this, the Samaritan put aside his own agenda, and he made himself vulnerable. The Samaritan also recognized that it would take time for the man to heal. He didn't expect him to recover overnight, and he made arrangements for the long recovery process, even to the point of starting a tab with the innkeeper that he would pay upon his return (v. 35).

As Christians, we often expect people who have just been "born again" or "saved" to be pure reflections of Jesus virtually overnight. But a relationship with God grows just like any other relationship. You may fall in love with someone, but then you spend the rest of your life getting to know that person and smoothing out the hard spots in the relationship along the way. Especially with offenders, who are grappling with the consequences of many painful life events and choices, we need to anticipate their need for plenty of time to heal and grow. Whether this is a criminal offender or a loved one or friend who is suffering (with no involvement in the justice system), we need to exercise kindness and patience, and give an open ear to listen when they want to talk. This isn't a call to ministry, but a reminder that if you know someone forgotten in prison, consider bringing them some encouragement through a card or letter.

As I healed, there were plenty of tears. And I can admit that I'm not a perfect Christian and I am certainly scarred by life's experiences. But I'm on the right road with God.

Though each of the chapters in this book is essentially a short story about the miraculous, saving work God has done in each offender's life, do not miss the months and years it took for each story to come to pass. What if I had listened to Zach's family, who had given up after years of helping him? What if I had given up after the first hour of canvassing the streets for Eddie on his bike? Faith, tenacity, and endurance are traits you rarely see in the pop-culture depictions of a detective's work.

When I start my day, I have no idea what kind of turn God has for me in a case. I'm not rubbing my hands together and consciously considering "How many souls can I pray for today?" But I certainly see my work as a ministry to others, because I get to go into those situations where only God knows what others bear.

That being said, ministering to, with, and for offenders is messy work. I bet the Samaritan and even his beast had some blood on them when they got to the inn. Similarly, when I am working on a case and interacting with offenders, I can feel the weight of the anger, depression, confusion, and sin that surround these men. A student once asked how I am able to relax and look at people normally when I am "off-duty," especially with my family. I told him that I purposefully take time to decompress and make the mental and physical transition between work and home. I do this by following Jesus' advice to his disciples in Matthew 10. Jesus said that if a disciple went to a home and the people there would not welcome him or listen to his words, that disciple was to take back his blessing of peace, leave, bang the dust off his sandals, and keep going. For me, the image of a dusty cloud of dirt and debris raining down from banging those sandals captures this transition from the street to home perfectly.

Most days I wear black boots, but I still metaphorically bang the dirt off and walk on when I make that transition from work to home. Sadly, I sometimes bang off the dirt and then have to walk into new dirt. I won't lie—sometimes the dirt feels like mud and it makes my steps very, very heavy.

I guarantee there are times when I feel heavy or tired or burned out. But feeling heavy or weary doesn't indicate a lack of faith. Even Jesus became weary (John 4:6). All physical and emotional weariness should simply direct us back to God for strength and encouragement. At one of David's lowest times, he encouraged himself in the Lord (1 Samuel 30:6). Being savvy enough to detect when we are tired or depressed or anxious, and then turning to God in prayer and other people for support, is a discipline that we grow into as Christians. In my line of work, I've had to pay close attention to such emotional heaviness, know when I need to bang the dust off my sandals, and encourage myself in God.

I believe that there are many reasons why you have chosen to read this book. It may have been curiosity about the detective business. You may have been seeking encouragement for others or for yourself. You may have been seeking understanding or a new way to view crime and offenders. My goal was to provide stories for encouragement and to highlight the themes of forgiveness.

If you know offenders or you are involved in working with this wide population of men and women who are suffering, who Jesus would describe as among "the least," please don't minister to earn points with God. Our salvation is based on God's grace through faith in Him alone and not on our works, so that we can't brag or take credit for our place in Heaven (Ephesians 2:8-9). Salvation is God's gift to us. If we minister to others, that love and compassion should be the natural outflow of our genuine faith and appreciation for what God has done for us (James 2:18). This is called the fruit of God's love.

The Samaritan did not give so sacrificially to the wounded man to impress others, inflate his own ego, or sway God to grant him access to Heaven. He gave because he cared about the man's well-being; he gave so the man might have a chance to live.

Though many offenders may serve a prison term set by months or years, others will spend the rest of their lives in prison, and still others are facing an uncertain countdown toward the death penalty. There is no delicate way to emphasize that life in prison is dangerous and full of risk. Life is in the balance, whether by the threat of execution or the reality of disease or a death by natural causes at a very old age. Prison is hell but God can help.

Keep this in mind: Jesus was born into poverty, lived as a roaming preacher, and died as a criminal. He deeply identifies with the shame and heartache these offenders feel, and he has compassion for them. He wants to bind up their wounds and heal their trauma. He is there for the offender and those who are suffering.

When I asked Jesus into my own heart, I never expected I would find myself in these situations. My mom's favorite scripture came back to me, and I can see more clearly a path intended for me: what we do for the least of our brothers and sisters, we do for God.

ABOUT THE AUTHOR

 Brian D. Baker has over twenty-five years of experience with professional investigation, security, and consulting. He has a master's degree in criminology from Vermont College, and he is an adjunct at Penn State University, where he teaches criminology and introduction to criminal justice. Brian is the author of several textbook chapters in the professional security and investigation industry, and he is a speaker at professional conferences. He lives with his wife, Michelle, and family in Central Pennsylvania. Brian is available for speaking engagements. To inquire about a possible appearance, please contact Morgan James Speaker's Bureau at www.themorganjamesspeakersgroup.com or visit www.detectivebaker.com.

Morgan James
Speakers Group

www.TheMorganJamesSpeakersGroup.com

We connect Morgan James published authors with live and online events and audiences whom will benefit from their expertise.

Printed in the USA
CPSIA information can be obtained
at www.ICGtesting.com
JSHW082344140824
68134JS00020B/1879

9 781683 502548